Keeping Track

Keeping Track

Success in Track and Field

By Robert C. Smith

Foreword by Joe Piane

Productivity Publications
3177 Latta Road #122
Rochester, NY 14612
585-392-3601

FIRST EDITION 2007

ISBN: 0-9729119-6-0
       978-0-9729119-6-2

Dedication

This book is dedicated to the memory of Elvin R. (Doc) Handy: coach, professor, friend, counselor, and confidant. I felt it an honor to have been on his last team before he departed from Notre Dame after nineteen years. He will live on in the hearts of "his boys."

Acknowledgments

In order for a track team to be successful, it has to have good athletes in all events. So it is with writing and publishing a book. Good people are necessary to contribute information that enables the author to do a creditable job.

"Keeping Track: Success in Track and Field" was edited by Kay Whipple, a difficult job well done.

One of our goals in producing this book was to provide a book that those with limited knowledge about track could enjoy. Don Barnbrook and Dave and Mary Szymczak offered suggestions on content. Pictures and/or recollections were provided by Dick Liechty, and my teammate, Paul Schwetshenau. Ray Brant and Richard Morrison helped me track down facts. I didn't have to go far to find a proofreader. My wife Candida did a great job as I went along. The rest of the family offered me encouragement: Kay, Eric, Phil, Jay, and their families.

Cheering along the home stretch and near the finish line were Chuck McGeath, Phil Harris, John Abell, Jay and Mary Ann Guy, Keith and Barb Carbiener, Ray Brant, Rich Blosser, Dottie and Augie Van Paris, Sam and Melba Holmgren, Bob Berger, John and Phyllis Clayton, Anita Glenn, Ron Bella, and Jim Peterson. A big "thank you" to everyone.

Credit should also be given to John Kovach at the Local History and Genealogy Department of the St. Joseph County (Indiana) Public Library, as well as Angie Kindig and Elizabeth Hogan at the University of Notre Dame Archives.

On a somber note, in April 2006, soon after providing his picture for this book, Bob Osborn passed away after an illness. During my tenure as coach at Riley High School, Bob was an assistant for three years.

Table of Contents

Foreword by Joe Piane *1*

Introduction *3*

Part I: My Athletic Career *7*

1 Disappointments of a Late Bloomer *9*

2 I Find my Niche *15*

3 Decisions, Decisions, Decisions *27*

4 Notre Dame Track *35*

5 The Olympic Trials *44*

6 The Climax *49*

7 Culmination of a Career *57*

Part II Coaching Track and Field *67*

8 The Dawn of a Coaching Career *69*

9 Track: The Basic and Best Sport *83*

10 Cross Country Coaching *93*

11 A Surprise Return *104*

Afterword *122*

Appendix A What is Track and Field ? *125*

Appendix B 1944 Central High School Track *131*

Appendix C 1945 Central High School Track *134*

Appendix D 1947-1950 Notre Dame Track *137*

Appendix E South Bend Riley H.S. Track *142*

Appendix F Riley High School Cross Country . . . *144*

Appendix G Notre Dame Track and Field Records *146*

About the Author *148*

Foreword

By Joe Piane, Head Track Coach, University of Notre Dame

Track and field is a great sport! It is an activity that all can enjoy because of its simple, yet graceful, nature. In fact, it is perhaps the world's first sporting event, dating back tens of thousands of years. The ancient Greeks used track and field (or "athletics," as it is known in international circles) as the foundation for the Olympic Games, which continues to be the world's greatest sporting celebration. The quick runner, the agile leaper, and the powerful thrower were revered as heroes and elevated to legendary status in a time when the only others to hold such exalted positions were scholars, philosophers, and perhaps even the Gods themselves.

If you look at the sport of track and field, you'll find it is completely unique in that almost any person can participate, regardless of height, weight, or skill level. The spectrum of track and field athletes is as diverse as the events within the sport itself, from the large 250-pound man who puts the shot, to the 100-pound woman who runs the 10,000 meters. If you have the desire to compete, your coach can find you an event.

Personally, I have seen track and field have a profound effect on student-athletes in all disciplines. Our student-athletes may not realize it at the time, but the structure and regimentation they go through during their college careers will have a positive effect on the rest of their lives..

One of our former student-athletes, who is a noted author today, has said that the discipline he learned through training is something he still uses in his work. On the track, we train daily in order to accomplish a goal. The same holds true for this author, as he now writes daily, whether inspired to do so or not, in order to maintain the work ethic and discipline needed to complete his next book.

Another former student athlete came to us as a fine runner with the goal of becoming a doctor. The lessons that he learned through track and field turned out to be beneficial in two ways: they not only created the framework for him to succeed as a runner on the national level, but they also proved to be critical in his pursuit of becoming an anesthesiologist. If not for the ideals and growth he gained through competing in our sport, he would not be where he is today.

An important component in this learning process is the coach, and I can think of no one who better embodies the word than Bob Smith. He's someone I would term a "gentleman coach," always there with an encouraging word or a friendly pat on the shoulder, just to let you know that you're doing just fine and he's right there beside you every step of the way. Coach Smith was a major contributor to the success of Notre Dame's track and field program during his tenure at the University, and for that we will be forever in his debt. Many student-athlete's benefited as competitors and individuals from Coach Smith's guidance. These student-athletes developed into successful runners on the track, but more importantly, they became successful human beings who continue to make significant contributions to society.

I am proud to call Coach Smith a colleague and a friend. It is through his long service and contribution to Notre Dame that our sport remains the great one it is today.

Introduction

I have brought myself by long meditation to the conviction that a human being with a settled goal must accomplish it, and that nothing can resist a will which will stake even existence upon its fulfillment.

Benjamin Disraeli, former Prime Minister of England

I grew up in the '30s and '40s, the decades before television, stereos, supermarkets, Little League sports, cell phones, and shopping malls, when two-car families were an extreme rarity. Those were the years of the Great Depression in the '30s, followed by World War II and Recovery in the '40s. Compared to what most of today's youngsters have, kids back then didn't have much. The thing was, no one was aware that they didn't have much. In many ways, growing up then was much like growing up now. Youngsters would dream of what they would like the future to bring and fantasize that the future was already here. I was no different.

During those formative years, I visualized doing all sorts of things, without regard to reality. I developed a liking for sports, and did what I could to develop this interest. In this book, I will follow the tortuous path through my athletic experiences, my attempts to follow my dreams and realize the fantasies that had been nurtured as I matured. It was a route that contained many disappointments. For every disappointment encountered, where one door closed, another opened. This wasn't evident at the time to a young kid, but every step along the way put me in contact with an adult who would have a profound influence on my life.

As my life played out, I found it was possible to meet my goals right here in South Bend, Indiana. While living at home on South Bend's northwest side, I received my education from kindergarten through college, all while living in the same house.

I wanted to be an athlete, and I became one. Perhaps when I started, what came my way wasn't what I visualized. Success came where I least expected it. In grade school, my experiences in basketball were abysmal, yet I can't look at it as a total failure. At least I found out what I *couldn't* do well. In high school, I discovered that my sport was track, and it was there that I excelled after so many disappointments. In this book, I tell the story of my journey from disappointment to a successful athletic experience.

I wanted to be a teacher, and I became one. I spent 39 years in the classroom in South Bend, 29 years at Riley High School and ten at Jackson High School. All but five of those years were spent teaching biology. My first five years of teaching were spent teaching seventh grade science at Riley, when Riley was grades 7 through 12. How successful was I as a teacher? That is not for me to say; each of my students had his/her experiences in my class. I'm sure they had a full range of opinions, from "he was super" to "couldn't stand him." I would tell my students not to judge their teachers until they had been out of class for five years, enough time to reflect and put the experience into perspective. Personally, the teachers that stand out in my memory are the ones who made me work the hardest and had dedication that showed they cared. I tried to emulate those teachers. How did I measure up? Ask the students.

One of my favorite teachers at Central was Miss Jeanne Gienand, my language teacher. I was in her class for two years of Spanish and one year of French. Now, there was one tough teacher (she also had a temper), but her dedication and love for the students shone through. I was "Roberto" for two years, and "Robert" (don't

4

pronounce the "t") for one. I remember one day when she really got upset with the class, she ended her tirade with the question "Who is crazy enough to become a teacher?" I was afraid to raise my hand. It's surprising how much Spanish and French I remember now, and I'm glad that SHE decided to become a teacher. I'm sure the class deserved the rebuke it got that day.

I wanted to be a coach, and I became one. When it came right down to it, my success in track got me interested in coaching. My interest in teaching came before that. Many people confuse the love of a sport with a love of coaching, and they really are not the same. After they have coached a while, they realize that is true.

Coaching is teaching, imparting knowledge and encouraging the athlete to apply it. A successful coach is also a good motivator, getting the athletes to push themselves on their own, wanting to do well themselves, and setting their own goals without being pushed by the coach.

The techniques of motivation are different for a track coach than for a football coach. The track coach deals more on the individual level, whereas the football coach works more on the team level. I have found that the thinking of a distance runner differs from that of a high jumper or a sprinter, and they require different handling. Because of the wide range of individuals in track, it helps if the coach has had personal track experience.

Coaching track is a challenging but rewarding experience. This book offers a glimpse behind the scenes of what it means to be a track coach on the high school and college level.

In this small volume, I examine the word "success," and I hope my understanding of it will encourage some to participate in those activities that interest them, and not be deterred by disappointments along the way.

What is success? How is it measured? How is it achieved? It should be easy to do in track, right? After all, either you beat the opposition or you do not. Wrong! A runner can be beaten decisively, but still run a personal best, overcoming personal obstacles to finish where he did. The winner of a particular race may have had great speed and skill, but underachieved through an unwillingness to work hard. Which athlete is more successful? "Success" and "failure" has to be measured on a *personal* basis.

Life is not measured by a turn around the track. It is measured in goals achieved, relationships forged, lives changed.

Was I successful? I had many disappointments along the way, but managed to do well beyond my wildest dreams. Yet in track, even when I was "on top," there were many runners I couldn't defeat. I had good meets and bad. I won some and lost more. Was I successful? You decide.

Part I: My Athletic Career

Ingenuity, plus courage, plus work, equals miracles.
Bob Richards, Pole Vaulter, Olympic Gold Medalist

Not everyone is born an athlete. For some it takes time to find the right sport, persistence to create success. This was the case for me. The road was long and the disappointments many, but in the end I found success beyond my imaginations.

1

Disappointments of a
Late Bloomer

Never give in.
Sir Winston Churchill, former Prime Minister of England

Every summer when I was a youngster, when I wasn't down on my grandparents' farm or at Boy Scout camp, you could find me lying in front of the radio, listening to Pat Flanagan or Bob Elson broadcasting the Cubs or White Sox games. As time went on, I would position my baseball cards to help me follow the game. (Don't ask me what happened to my baseball cards.) I knew every player on every team, a feat that was made easier by the fact there were only eight teams in each league. Due to the success of the Cubs in the '30s and the fact that I liked Pat Flanagan as an announcer better than Bob Elson (who covered the Sox), I became a Cubs fan, a malady that persists to this day. I understand there is no cure. Using my imagination to follow the game on the radio, I'd fantasize about becoming a good athlete. As a Cubs fan, my dreams and fantasies really got a workout.

My hands-on experience as a ballplayer came during the ball games that were played in the street in front of our house almost every evening. There were enough neighborhood kids to form what might pass for two teams. Home plate was the manhole cover in front of our next-door neighbor's house. First base was the water valve access, second was a patch of asphalt, and third was a piece of plywood that one of the kids brought. We lived a couple blocks from the Drewrys Brewery, and the beer trucks exiting the brewery used our street. Many times the game had to be stopped to allow the passage of a big beer truck. Looking back, it is a miracle that someone didn't put a ball through a window or get run down by a beer truck, but no one ever did. Looking at today's Little League programs, we were certainly a deprived group. No one knew it, so everyone had a good time.

In grade school, I had no opportunity to play organized ball, which accounted for the spirited games in the street. There was one opportunity to compete, the annual Sunday School picnic, which was held in a local park. The picnic always had a good turnout, since church and school activities played an important role in the social lives of the Depression-weary folks. Despite the hard times, we had plenty of good food and fun activities for all. It was at just such a gathering as this that I had my first competitive success at the age of nine.

"All you kids under 12, get over here by this line. It's time for the foot race! You start here, race down to that big tree, circle the tree, and finish here where you started. Everyone ready – get set – GO!"

I was off and ran like the wind down to the big tree, grabbed the tree so I could get around it, and headed for the finish line – all alone. I won easily, the first race I ever won. I went to the table to claim my prize. It was a chartreuse baseball cap. It wasn't really what I had in mind, but I wasn't about to turn it down. It would be quite a while before I would run a competitive race again, and it was the last race where I would have to circle a tree.

Elementary School Woes

I went to Muessel School in South Bend, Indiana, from kindergarten through my freshman year. Muessel's teams were the Cardinals, and their school colors were red and white.

When I entered the fifth grade, I decided it was time for me to make my move in school athletics and go out for the fifth grade basketball team. Unfortunately, it seemed that half the male population of fifth graders had the same idea. I wasn't very tall, was slight of build (scrawny!) and wasn't coordinated. It was hardly surprising that Coach Volney Wier didn't notice me. It didn't take long to stake out my home-away-from-home at the end of the bench. I didn't get cut, however, and had high hopes of making the traveling squad to our big game with Colfax School, just a few blocks away. It was not to be. I was one of the few not to make the traveling squad, even though "traveling" meant that everyone walked to Colfax. I didn't even make that group! That was a real downer, but the season soon ended and not a moment too soon.

In sixth grade, I gave basketball another shot. When practice began, I found that little had changed. I was still short, uncoordinated, and scrawny, and I think Coach Wier had the same opinion of me as an athlete.

A big thing happened to me during the season, however. We had a big game with Harrison School (one of the best in town) and I *made the traveling squad!* Harrison School was located on the western side of South Bend, about two miles from Muessel. When game day arrived, it was very snowy, making travel difficult. I soon found out why several of us probably made the traveling squad. After Harrison routed our team and it was time to go home, we found that it took everyone present to push the coaches' cars out of the snowdrifts. Now, Coach Wier was a nice upright man, and I dismissed out of mind the idea that he took us along just to push

11

him out. It only seemed so at the time. I didn't get to play in the game, either.

Junior High Fiasco

Sixth grade passed into seventh: junior high. Surely after having a two-year stay on the end of the bench, my growing skills would have to become apparent to Coach Dresbach, the junior high coach. Apparently not. This time I lost my lease on the end of the bench. When the list of those who would continue in basketball was posted, I looked in vain for my name. My career in basketball was over. In my two years on the basketball team, I did not get into even one game.

The junior high coach, Robert Dresbach, was an excellent basketball, football, and baseball coach. Muessel was a feeder school for Central High School, and Coach Dresbach developed many of the players who would help in the Central Bears' success. I failed to detect, however, much of an interest in track, and suspect that track was something that just got in the way of baseball. In fairness to Coach Dresbach, South Bend did not have much of a junior high track program. It didn't matter anyway.

Junior high track turned out to be another disappointment. When it came time to choose the junior high team, the boys' gym classes lined up at one end of the playground and raced to the other. The first few boys who reached the other end made the team. The number chosen varied, depending on the speed of the fastest ones. Where was I? Back in the pack, and that was the end of junior high track for me.

Lessons I Never Wanted... and Lessons I Did

While I was spending my time still fantasizing about becoming a ballplayer, my mother was coming up with some ideas of her own about how I should be spending my time. She wanted me to develop my cultural side, which, up to that point, didn't exist. I'm sure most mothers go through this phase and most succeed to some degree. My mother wanted me to take piano lessons. This idea didn't meet with my immediate approval.

My teacher would be a lady who lived in the next block. I saw that I was going to lose this one, so I reluctantly agreed to the piano lessons, not realizing that I had to pay for the lessons by mowing the teacher's lawn. Paying for lessons I really didn't want didn't thrill me. I was experienced in lawn care already, since I mowed our own lawn, and had another one on the next street to keep mowed and trimmed as well. The going rate for a cut and trim was fifty cents. That's right, fifty cents. That was decent pay at the time. It didn't take long to determine that I was not going to be a virtuoso on the piano. Looking back, I wasn't motivated to practice hard enough to improve. My attitude was typical of many young people who were pushed into taking music lessons when their heart wasn't in it.

Mom's next project was to convince me that I needed to take ballroom dancing lessons. Now *there* was an activity I was going to resist. I was very shy around girls in junior high and was really half-afraid of them. No, I wasn't going to take dancing. My buddy, Howard Gindelberger, was of the same mind. We would fight this one out together. What we didn't count on was that our mothers would get together. The two of them informed us that we *were* going to dancing class, so off to dancing class we went.

The thing I remember most was that when we paired off with a partner, mine was taller than I was, and when I looked straight ahead, all I could see was her belt buckle. I was very self-conscious, and never really did learn to dance. Howie fared better, and he learned to enjoy dancing. Although I went to several school dances, I was never very comfortable because I was a lousy dancer.

When I was in the 9th grade, I was asked to be a substitute for an older friend, John Zeitler, delivering his South Bend Tribune route on those rare days when he couldn't. It wasn't long before I was offered my own route. It was on Portage Avenue from Kessler

Blvd. to the cemetery plus Woodlawn Ave. It was a difficult route to deliver because the houses were farther apart and farther back from the sidewalk. It was one of the least desirable routes to deliver, although the customers were very nice. One of the problems was the route was one of the farthest from the paper station where we picked up our papers. I worked my way up to a route on Diamond, Cleveland, Vassar, and California Avenues. This route was closer to home and the porches were easier to hit with the papers since they were closer to the sidewalk. I kept delivering papers for over two years. It afforded me a nice income, and it introduced me to the world of meeting responsibilities.

Looking back, carrying papers was one of the best things I ever did. I had 93 customers and delivered the papers by bicycle, throwing the folded paper on each porch from the sidewalk as I rode along. Occasionally I would "roof one," which would then pose a problem, because then I had to come up with another paper. When I had a good day, I would be able to finish the entire route in 20 minutes.

One noteworthy thing happened while I had the route: South Bend hit its all-time low temperature one Sunday morning. It was 23 degrees below zero with heavy snow, and I had to deliver the route on foot. That's something you don't soon forget.

The Glee Club

While I was at Muessel, I was in the Glee Club. I wasn't much of a singer, but I blended in and enjoyed most of the songs. The teacher was Ruby Guilliams, and no one messed around in her class. I really liked Miss Guilliams and had the privilege of teaching with her when I taught high school. It was always "Miss Guilliams," never "Ruby." Miss Guilliams commanded the type of respect that did not lend itself to calling her by her first name, although I don't think she would have minded.

2

I Find my Niche

Anyone can get good results from a physically perfect individual who is forced into a scientific training regime. The beauty comes when someone who is imperfect has great desire and as a result achieves great results.
Emil Zatopek, Distance Runner and Olympic Gold Medalist

Following the ninth grade, I moved on to Central High School, where I graduated in May, 1945. The Central Bears wore orange and blue. Central gained some fame for losing to a small-town team in the movie *Hoosiers*. REAL Hoosiers know the movie got the team colors wrong.

Now that I was in high school, I had an opportunity to play on our church's softball team. Since it was during the war, skilled players were scarce. Most teams consisted of older men and teenagers so it gave a youngster like me a chance to play. I hate to draw the analogy, but our church team was comparable to the Cubs of the same period. (The winning 1945 season was unusual for the Cubs.) The few times we won, it was because the other team was worse. Our team had one pitcher, and you could read the writing on his fast ball as it made its way to the plate. It's a good thing most games were played before dark because many balls would have been hit beyond the range of the lights. We needed a fleet outfield, and we didn't have it. Most of the time, I played in the outfield, where much of the action was. Whenever I played in the infield, my erratic throwing arm was a liability. No one knew just where the throw would go. Batting was not my forte, either.

One of the teams we played was Second Church of the Brethren. They had a good team, including one of the best pitchers in town, Keith Carbiener. Keith attends our church now, and we are friends. We laugh together when I mention that I don't think I ever got a good foul ball when batting against him. Thanks to him and many others, my ballplaying career didn't progress very far.

There was also a Church Basketball League and I played on our church's team. The only time I got in the game was when they needed a fifth player. That was okay because my homeroom at Central had an intramural team, which turned out to be a poor one because the rest of the team had the same level of skill that I had. The other teams looked forward to playing Room 304 for obvious reasons and were seldom disappointed. My chances of becoming a decent athlete were fading. I had made the most of what I had amidst the shambles of my athletic dreams, but life was about to change.

A Change in Direction

After my first year at Central, two things happened that took me out of music. First my voice changed, which eliminated me as an asset in any vocal group. Second, I was expected to be in the school play, which ruined any day in which I thought about it. I was a very shy, self-conscious teenaged lad, and when I was on the stage, I thought everyone was looking at me. The play was *The Devil and Daniel Webster*. As one of the cast of thousands that filled the stage, I spent most of my time hiding behind the scenery. I felt very self-conscious up on the stage in front of all those people.

Now, Central had an outstanding music and drama department, and I thought if it was to continue, it had better do without me. I envisioned at least two more school plays, and that just wasn't going to happen to me. Miss Helen Weber was the music teacher, and she didn't take it lightly when anyone left. That's one reason why she was such a good teacher. She finally agreed that if I would substitute something else, she would let me out. I told her I was going out for the track team, and that got me out of the glee club. That decision led me to Bert Anson, who changed my life.

Bert Anson was a high school history teacher. He had taught in several schools in South Bend. When I was a junior, he happened to be at Central. He was also a coach, having coached various sports at the high school and junior high school level. The important thing is that he was a high school teacher coaching track, rather than a coach teaching history. As time went on and it was apparent that I was going to become a teacher and coach, Bert's teaching and coaching philosophy took on greater meaning to me. Teacher first, coach second. I tried to apply what I had learned from Bert into my own teaching and coaching situation. In addition to his philosophies, he was also a very knowledgeable coach, and he knew how to pass on what he knew. What made him a good teacher also made him a good coach. I was sorry to see him transfer after my junior year. After he earned his doctorate, he finished his career as a history professor at Ball State University.

One morning before the start of school, I went to Bert's classroom to sign up for track. There were several members of the track team around his desk, absorbing what they could from him, but more than likely it was just a social time. I introduced myself to Bert and explained what I would like to do. He greeted me warmly and told me when and where the first practice would be held. I felt that he really wanted me out there, which amazed me because I was an inexperienced junior who had never seen a track meet, let alone run in one. Elated, I made up my mind to do the very best possible.

Track practice was held in the basement of Central High School. Central was located in downtown South Bend and had no outdoor athletic facilities. The track we used was located inside the football stadium, School Field, located a good mile away. We had two indoor meets scheduled, but they would be too early for us to use the outdoor track, so we practiced in the school basement. The basement had a wooden floor that wasn't *too* hard on our legs. Bert estimated that running one lap around the basement would be close to a 220. It turned out that all of our practices before our first meet were held in the basement.

Bert determined that I would run the 440, the quarter mile. I had no idea what running the quarter would be like, since I had never run one, nor seen one run in a meet. I would soon find out.

The day of the first meet finally arrived. Indoor meets at that time were run in the old Notre Dame field house. Although it was old, it contained an excellent clay 220 banked track: two laps to the quarter, eight to the mile. The opposition, Fort Wayne North, had already arrived and was warming up in their nice red warm-ups. Whether they were good or not, it didn't matter. They looked good. As it turned out, they *were* good. At this point, my memory fails on most details of the meet, including the score. I do remember it wasn't even close. The Bears were routed. The hometown team was clad in their old practice sweat clothes of sweat suit gray, which, as it turns out, would serve us the rest of the season and the next one too. Fashion plates we weren't. We had to allow our performances to speak for us. At this first meet, the performances of some matched their attire. Mine did.

Never having run the 440 before, I took a couple practice laps to get the feel of the track. After a proper warm-up, I was ready to go when the event was announced. I took my place in the front row of runners. We answered the command: "Take your mark," followed by "get set," and a second later by the report of the starter's pistol. We were off, and I headed for the first turn. Coming out of the first turn, I found that I was leading. I was feeling relaxed, moving nicely, and maintaining a short lead throughout the first lap. Heading into the second lap, I was getting a little tired, but by the time I got to the backstretch of the second lap, I began to lose feeling in my legs and my arms felt numb. I made it into the last turn, and by the time I reached about 10 yards from the finish, I didn't feel a thing. The next thing I knew, Coach Anson was picking me up off the track. I had passed out before finishing my first race!

To say this was a disappointment doesn't do the word justice. Track was to have been my sport! The sport that hard work would pay off with success. My first official effort produced this result. I was finished.

Then Bert Anson stepped in. The next day he cornered me and talked with me. I was in no mood to run the quarter anymore, but Bert said that in the next meet he was going to put me in the 880 yard relay, where each runner runs a 220. My first 440 turned out to be my last 440 run in high school. Bert knew exactly what to say to this disappointed kid, and in the process, he saved my career.

Later, when running for Notre Dame, I would run the mile relay (each runner a 440) in some of the largest meets in the country, and in one indoor meet against Indiana University, I ran the open quarter, tying for first place with teammate Bob Boyne. All this happened because a teacher-turned-coach knew how to handle a disappointing situation with one of his inexperienced charges.

When the indoor season was completed, it was time to move outdoors. This was received with mixed emotions, because early March in northern Indiana is usually cold and blustery. School Field was not the most hospitable place in early spring, and it was far from school. The locker room, located under the northern stands, was next to impossible to heat properly, so it did not lend itself to socializing. It was all about getting in, showering, and getting out. Of course, when spring finally did arrive, the sense of urgency wasn't so great.

The track itself left plenty to be desired. It was a cinder track that could never be compacted enough to provide a firm surface, although the School Field maintenance man, Mike Zalas, did his best. Not only did he do his best with the track, but also the locker room. He just didn't have much to work with. Our jumping pits were nothing more than spaded sand. A drop of eleven feet into one of those pits was quite a jolt to the system.

Up through the 1940s, cinder tracks were found everywhere I ran. Over the years there has been a vast improvement in tracks, pits, shoes, and equipment, notably vaulting poles. I often wonder what the times, heights, and distances would have been back then if we'd had the composition track surfaces and the jumping pits that are available today OR what the times would be today if the athletes had to use only what was available to us back then.

Bert Anson worked his team hard getting ready for the first outdoor meet, experimenting with different people in different events, a never-ending scenario for all coaches. During this process, he found that I had a natural talent for running the low hurdles, and if Bert had been there my senior year, running the low hurdles would have been on my list of things to do.

Interestingly, late in my senior year at Notre Dame, Coach Doc Handy had room in the 220 lows against Bradley and Monmouth, and he put me in at the last minute. I hadn't practiced the hurdles at all and didn't do well. I would have been all right if the race had been on a straightaway instead of around a curve. All that little episode proved was that Doc carried out a threat (he knew I had the talent for it), and the rest of the team had a good laugh.

1944 High School Races

During the 1944 season, my first, we had a state-caliber low hurdler, Joe Mathews, who indeed got to the state finals. Joe was also fast enough to beat me in the 100 more often than not. That season, Joe Mathews ran the 100 yard dash and low hurdles, and I ran the 100 and 220 yard dashes.

The first race I ever won in high school was the 100 yard dash in a meet with Riley High School. I was very nervous before the race and later found that being nervous before ANY race was a good thing. Running the race with an adrenaline charge enabled me to run faster. I concentrated on the race, although there wasn't time to think about anything except the fastest competitor. Given a choice, I liked to run in the lane next to my biggest competitor, which helped me to work harder in practice or in a meet. It always helped to know where he was. I assumed that I had to be in better shape, both physically and mentally, to win, since I knew the competition was aiming for the same goal. Later, when coaching, I found that we won many meets, particularly in cross country, simply by being in better condition than the opposition.

The Adams meet was the first of many confrontations with Lou McKinney from Adams High School, a tough competitor and a fine person. Competing over the course of a season and career with the likes of Lou McKinney makes track the sport it is. Not only do you compete, but you also get to know your rivals: how they think, the strategies they use, how to make it to the finish line in front of them, and how to lose graciously to them. These skills are useful in later life.

Central, along with the other South Bend schools, competed in the Northern Indiana Conference, which consisted of Eastern and Western Divisions. There was a qualifying meet in each division, which was followed by the large conference meet. The Northern Indiana has always been a very competitive conference.

I was very pleased to place second in both sprints in the Eastern Division meet. It was my finest effort of the year, and my performance gave me confidence for the future. It was an accomplishment to get that far my first year on the team.

However, it was obvious by the results of the Northern Indiana Conference Finals that I was not ready for prime time. I was outclassed and outrun. This kind of meet can be called a learning experience.

The State Sectional was the qualifying meet for the state track championships. This meet had nothing to do with the Conference meets. Each school was allowed two entrants in each event. An athlete did not have to qualify for the Sectional, just be entered by his school. The top two finishers in each event qualified for the state finals in Indianapolis.

Our sectional meet was held in Mishawaka. Back when I was in school, an athlete went straight from the Sectional to the State meet. Today he goes to the Regional and Semi-state before the state final.

This Sectional meet definitely qualified as a disappointment, because I finished third in the 100, and we were simply outrun in the 880 relay. The disappointment had to be put into perspective. When the season started back in February, just running in the Conference and Sectional had seemed out of reach, but not only had I gone, but I had placed. Over the season, success had enticed me to raise the bar of my expectations. That season, I was able to score enough points for a monogram award.

Looking at the 1944 season (see Appendix B for more details), it was clear that we didn't have enough depth to have a good team. I really didn't assess the season as a whole, since I was too inexperienced. All I thought about was doing the best I could, and afterward tried to sort out who would be coming back, both on our team and the opposition. We would improve in 1945, but we would sorely miss Joe Mathews. Considering that we only won one meet in 1944, there was plenty of room for improvement.

The 1945 Season

In the 1945 team election for captain, quarter miler Bill Yoder and I were selected as co-captains. It was an honor, not to be taken lightly. The only downer for the season was hearing over the summer that Coach Anson had been transferred to South Bend Washington as a history teacher. His replacement as track coach at Central was the assistant football coach, Jack Nash. Coach Nash had played football at Indiana University, and his track knowledge was limited. He had a very different approach than Bert Anson, and we were all concerned about how things would work out. We needn't have worried, since we had a very fine season in 1945. Detailed results for 1945 are in Appendix C.

As the record shows, 1945 was a turnaround for Central. We didn't lose any dual or quadrangular meets. We didn't run into trouble until we got to the big meets. Our improvement can be attributed to the improvement of Chuck Neises in the distances, Dick Chandonia's improvement in the shot and hurdles, and my improvement in the sprints. Both Chuck and Dick went to the state meet in 1945.

We also had a promising 880 relay team, which Coach Nash put together at the beginning of the season and kept together in the same order all season. Good move. Don Newman, Dick Taylor, and I were all holdovers from the prior year. Don Schleuder, a gifted athlete from the swim team and the Tumbling Club, proved to have enough speed to become the fourth man in the relay. The relay team's speed gave us the goal of getting to the state finals. Our inexperience led to mishaps that cost us two disqualifications when the baton was exchanged outside the zone. The disqualification that hurt most was in the Eastern Division Conference, which cost us fourth place in the meet. If we were to compete against the best, we had to make full use of the exchange zone and make our exchanges at full speed, which meant the exchanges had to take place near the end line of the exchange zone. It took most of the season to get it right. At the Sectional 880 relay, we ended up running just off our best time of the season and winning. We were off to the state meet.

Bob Smith, Don Schleuder, Dick Taylor, Coach Jack Nash, Chuck Neises, and Don Newman *Photo courtesy of the South Bend School Corporation*

This journey was not without some anxious moments, though. World War II was winding down. Germany surrendered on May 6, 1945, but the war continued against Japan and the draft was still in effect. At this stage of the war, everyone drafted went into the army, since the Battle of the Bulge had produced a need to replenish the army's ranks. If anyone wanted the navy or marines, he had to enlist before turning 18. I preferred the navy and enlisted, because my birthday was on May 26th. I was sworn into the navy in Indianapolis the Wednesday before the Sectional on Friday, and it wasn't certain if I would be allowed to come home. I was sent home, however, much to my relief, as well as the relief of Jack

Nash and my teammates. My presence set the stage for us to win the 880 relay and go on to the state meet.

In addition to the relay, I also qualified for two sprints: the 100 and 220. Newman qualified  for the 100. Neither of us got beyond the qualifying round, as neither of us was fast enough to compete at that level individually. The Indiana state champion in the sprints that year was Paul Bienz from Fort Wayne. Paul went on to run at Tulane, and we competed against each other several times, always with the same result. I never came close. Paul and I did get to know each other.

Don Pettie and Paul Bienz

In the 880 relay by the time the baton got to me, we were already third, and I had no chance of catching anyone. We ended third, the middle of the pack. We'd been beaten by the best, beating those behind us. Were we disappointed? Of course, but yet we accomplished a feat unexpected at the beginning of the season, and certainly unexpected by the junior that Bert Anson picked up off the track the year before. But wait! The best was yet to come.

At graduation each year, the Kiwanis Club made an award to each sport based on scholarship, citizenship, and sportsmanship. This award was given in each of the four South Bend high schools in football, basketball, baseball, and track. A grand award was chosen from one of the individual winners. I was the Kiwanis Award winner for track for Central High School, but John Brademas won the grand award that year. His sport was football, and he played quarterback at Central.

John Brademas became a Rhodes Scholar. He served several terms as the US Congressman from our district, and became quite influential in the House. After serving in Congress, he became the president of New York University. The South Bend Post Office is named after him now. At our last high school reunion, he and I had a long chat. He is a very down-to-earth person.

3
Decisions, Decisions, Decisions

An intelligent plan is the first step to success. The man who plans knows where he is going, knows what progress he is making and has a pretty good idea when he will arrive. Planning is the open road to your destination. If you don't know where you are going, how can you expect to get there?

Basil S. Walsh, businessman

The two years after I graduated from high school were filled with decisions that would affect the rest of my life. During transitional times, a person gets down to the foundations of what is most important and meaningful: how one can best serve mankind.

Finding Direction in the Navy

On June 6, 1945, I entered the Navy and served on active duty until July 20, 1946. During my time in the Navy, I served on the USS Ranger, an aircraft carrier. The Ranger was the first carrier in the Navy built from the keel up as a carrier. The other carriers that started World War II were converted cruisers. The war against Japan ended in August with the dropping of the atomic bombs. I can't help but wonder what my future would have been if the bombs hadn't been dropped. The invasion of Japan had been scheduled for November, and I would have been a part of it.

During the time I was in the navy, I made the decision to become a teacher and coach. I had been so impressed with my track coaches up until then, and so admired my classroom teachers, that I decided to follow in their footsteps. This was an admirable goal, and one that could be achieved. With the war over, it wouldn't be too long before I was discharged. Earlier, I had applied to Notre Dame. The problem was that I didn't know if I would be accepted or if I'd be discharged in time to start the fall semester.

Enter George Cooper: a man well known and well respected in South Bend. George Cooper was the long-time physical director at the South Bend YMCA and camp director at Camp Eberhart. He was also the starter at most of the major track meets in the area, so he had a chance to see me run, especially during my senior year. Perhaps he saw my potential, for my times did not warrant any interest on his part.

Coop was a long-time bachelor, and there just happened to be a very attractive widow living right next door to us. Somehow they met, and a courtship began which culminated in marriage. Coop spent enough time next door for us to get to know him.

After finding that I would be discharged in July, and able to start the fall semester, George Cooper "walked" my application through the application process, since he was also a professor at Notre Dame. With his help, I was able to start Notre Dame in the fall semester, 1946, and the next big adventure began.

After his marriage, Coop moved into a house he owned a couple blocks away, and during my senior year, I walked over and rode out to Notre Dame with him. On October 26, 1965, the Indiana Legislature named a bridge after him. The rebuilt Sample Street Bridge became the Cooper Bridge.

Financial Decisions

Now that I was an official student at Notre Dame, it was time to make some decisions. How was I going to pay for my education? Having served in the navy, I qualified for the GI Bill, but hadn't served long enough for benefits to cover all four years. It was determined that I would have enough benefits to cover tuition for only three years. I would be responsible for room and board, books, and everyday expenses. My own assets consisted of what I'd saved before I went into the navy and what I was able to save while in the navy. The sum was not large, and I found that I could get by more cheaply by living at home, eating breakfast and supper at home, having lunch at school, and paying bus fare to and from Notre Dame. I did not have a car. The decision was made easier by the fact that the dorms were filled by the time I arrived. With my limited GI Bill, I would pay my way with my limited savings, working during vacations and during school in the dining hall if need be. I would make it. I even had the means to go out for the track team as a walk on athlete.

After being out for the team for a few weeks and showing enough potential to the coach, Elvin (Doc) Handy, things began to break for me. Since I had worked very hard and was able to beat several sprinters he already had, Doc figured he might have something here. One afternoon he asked me if I needed any help. After explaining my situation to him, he offered me a meal ticket for lunch and supper. I was elated, and this bonus solved a big problem for me. Now I would be able to eat supper after practice in the evening before I came home. The evening meal was at the training table, which was a late line with extra food. Things were also looking up on the track, and by the end of the season, I had won a monogram as a freshman, thus vindicating Doc's faith in me. Doc was a person that one didn't ever want to let down.

Working vacations and summers provided the funds for books, bus fare, and spending money. One summer I worked at the South Bend Bait Company, fixing reels that needed repairs. Another summer was spent at the Post Office, carrying a route for vacationing regulars. Another year, I was a laborer, helping build houses. During Christmas vacations, I worked at the Post Office as holiday help. When my GI Bill ran out at the end of my junior year, I was awarded an athletic scholarship covering tuition and meals. I was able to finance my four years at Notre Dame and compete on the track team as well. That experience was successful beyond my wildest dreams. The disappointments of fifth grade basketball were not even on the chart.

Academic Options

Wanting to become a teacher and coach, I was unsure of an academic major. Notre Dame, as a national university, had a teaching program that met the requirements of all 50 states. Not having much counseling, I enrolled in the School of Physical Education because some places required it for coaches. Upon arriving on campus and learning about the various programs, I decided I didn't want to be a gym teacher, but would rather be a history teacher. I went to see Dr. John Scannell, head of the Physical Education Department, to change from P.E. to the History Department. Dr. Scannell, affectionately known as "Big John," pointed out to me that if I did that, all I would be able to teach would be history, but if I stayed in Physical Education, I would have enough required courses to qualify for licenses in physical education, health, and biology. Electives could be taken to qualify for history. As it turned out, I stayed in P.E. and earned 30 history hours. This important decision paved the way for five years teaching general science and 34 years as a biology teacher.

Favorite Professors

When I think of the teachers I had at Notre Dame, I feel that most of them were outstanding and met the needs of the students. I was also surprised that I had most of my best professors during my freshman year. I'm sure that didn't happen by accident.

Dr. Scannell was an outstanding teacher and taught several of my courses in the Physical Education school. He was a giant among his peers and certainly served as a role model for those aspiring to be teachers. His main contribution was that of teaching organization and study habits. He was a very disciplined man, and it came through in his teaching.

Dr. Cecil Birder, my speech teacher, was involved with music and drama. He was very good at drawing out shy and quiet people and getting them used to speaking in front of people – exactly what I needed.

My English composition teacher, Dr. Thomas Madden, was very friendly and laid back. He made the students very comfortable with the English language as he taught writing skills. He would assign one paper a week which incorporated what we had been learning. He worked us hard, but we weren't aware of it.

Dr. Willis Nutting taught history. His class was very different. There was no text. All we had were the notes we took in class, and we were tested on them. Better not miss any classes and better pay attention. I certainly honed my note taking skills in his class.

My freshman biology teacher was Dr. Donald Plunkett. This was my only class with lectures in an amphitheater. There were around 100 in the class, yet he knew everyone's name. Outside of class, he was referred to as "Flunk it with Plunkett" in an affectionate way. He was a good teacher because he kept us on our toes.

One teacher I had in the Physical Education Department was Francis Maxwell. He taught both gym classes and classroom courses, and he was good both places. I had absolutely no gymnastic experience before coming to Notre Dame, and Francis Maxwell introduced me (and most of the rest of the class) to gymnastics and tumbling. I'm glad his paycheck didn't depend on how well we performed. A few in the class were very skilled – and then there were the rest of us. He was a very good classroom teacher, also. I remember that in one class we discussed financing of high school athletics. In most states, tax money could not be spent to support athletics, except for facilities and coaches' pay. Maxwell disagreed with that, taking the position that if athletics was important enough to be part of the school program, then it should be supported by taxes, just like English and math. He made a strong case for it, and I tended to agree with him.

I cannot remember having any poor teachers at Notre Dame, although one course (psychology) was hard for me to follow and understand. Although I passed, I didn't take much from the course. I suspect it was more my fault than the teacher's.

Religious Choices

I am not a Catholic. I was born and raised a Presbyterian and continue to be one to this day. When I got my class schedule for the first semester, it included religion, so I had to go. At the end of the first class, the priest said that if any non-Catholic students would rather not stay, they should see him. I did.

The priest asked if I went to church.

"Yes," I answered.

"Where?" he asked.

"Westminster Presbyterian in South Bend," I answered.

"How often do you go?" he asked.

"Every week," I responded.

The priest then agreed to write me out of the class. He wished me well, and I thanked him. Although I was not a Catholic, all of my contacts with the clergy were very positive. I had a very enjoyable course in Aristotle's Ethics taught by Father Leo Ward. Father Ward was one of the legends of the University, and I was very glad to have been in one of his classes.

Twelve hours of religion were required to graduate. If you were excused from religion, twelve hours of something else had to replace them. I substituted history for religion, and that is how I was able to accumulate so many hours in history. A 3-hour history class substituted for a 2-hour religion class. It was a heavier academic load for me, but well worth it.

Time Management Decisions

Living at home presented several problems for me, some of which should be obvious. Getting to campus in time to meet my early classes was one problem. I had eight o'clock classes six days a week for all four years, and that included Saturdays. Some of my classes met on Monday, Wednesday, and Friday, and others on Tuesday, Thursday, and Saturday. Once I got on campus, I was there for the day and had the problem of filling the occasional time gap between classes. I took advantage of open periods by studying and doing homework, either in the library or in a classmate's room for an hour. By careful management of my time during the day, I was able to reduce the amount of work to do in the evening. Being organized and disciplined was essential, since I needed to fit in trips to track meets. The study habits learned at Notre Dame stood me in good stead throughout my teaching career.

Following practice was dinner, and then it was time to head for home. I got there around eight p.m. and had a three-block walk home from the bus stop. The rest of the evening was spent doing homework. Bedtime was never later than midnight.

Soon after the semester began, I got a big break. I found that a Notre Dame professor, Lee Daniel, lived just down the street from me. He was more than happy to pick me up in the morning and take me to school. Not only did this solve my transportation problem (especially in the winter), but Lee Daniel came into my life. Every morning a little after seven, I would go out to the corner, and Lee would pick me up. This happened for three years. My senior year Lee Daniel had a change in schedule, so I rode out with George Cooper, who now lived three blocks away.

Lee Daniel was an engineering drawing professor. He was originally from Iowa, and before coming to Notre Dame he had taught high school and coached basketball at various schools in north central Iowa. I loved spending time with Lee. I would go to his house, and we would sit and talk. I can still see him sitting in his favorite chair, smoking his pipe, and generally serving as an idol for the kid down the block. We would talk about the Cubs, fly fishing, the sad state of the world, and occasionally, the topic even got around to track. He was an avid fly fisherman and made his own flies. He even taught me how. He and his lovely wife, Dorothy, had a cabin on a river up in Wisconsin near Gleason, and that's where they spent their summers.

Lee was a homebody's homebody. He spent most of his time at home and wouldn't even attend our home track meets. He always seemed to know about them, though. The only time he showed any excitement about track was the time I went down to see him after I ran a :09.6 100 yard dash at Bradley University. Before going to see Lee, I called to see if he was available. He was, and when I got there, he was sitting on the bottom porch step waiting for me. I cried when he died in 1984.

4
Notre Dame Track

Our proudest boast at Notre Dame is that all of our athletes also become well educated and that quality shows itself in their later lives.

Reverend Theodore M. Hesburgh C.S.C.,
University of Notre Dame President

Once classes started and I'd settled into my academic routine, it was time to get out for fall track. When I went to check in

with Doc Handy, he gave me a note requesting equipment and directed me to the equipment manager, Jack McAllister, over at the field house. Now, every athlete who ever went to Notre Dame during the tenure of "Mac" have their stories to tell concerning Mac, and I would not doubt the truth of any of them. Mac delighted in giving All-American football players a hard time. You can imagine how he would feast on a freshman track walk-on.

Jack McAllister *photo by Paul Schwetshenau*

Mac could be very profane, and he had a variety of names he applied to anybody and everybody. He used some words for the team producers, and other words for athletes who weren't so productive. I remember how thrilled I was when I made it to the "word."

My first contact with Mac went something like this:

Mac: "What do you want kid?"
Bob: "Here is a note from Doc asking you to give me equipment."
Mac: "Get the #### out of here."
Bob: "But I need equipment to practice!"
Mac: "Are you a freshman?"
Bob: "Yes."
Mac: "You will never make it anyway, so get the #### out of here.

Believe it or not, this went on for almost a week. I finally went to Doc, and he personally went with me and made Mac give me the equipment. You should have seen the socks he gave me! They had holes in them so big that I didn't know where to put my foot. This went on and on, and one year stretched into another, and then another. The edge was off a little bit by the time I experienced success on the track, and by the time senior year came around, Mac gave me my uniform running shirt and shorts and my last pair of spikes, which were practically new. I still have them. He said he would like to give me the meet warm-up uniform, but he didn't have enough as it was. I believed him. One might say his bark was worse than his bite, and long-term that was right, but try telling that to a shy freshman trying to get equipment!

Finally, on the team

Finally after all the preliminaries, I got out for fall track and was able to meet some of my new teammates. It was interesting to discover where their homes were. Notre Dame is truly a national university. The sprinters and quarter milers in the fall of 1946 were Dave Murphy from Illinois, Ernie McCullough from Calgary, Alberta, Canada, Brad Bennett from California, Paul Schwetshenau from Ohio, Steve Provost from Bronx, New York, Ray Sobota from Pennsylvania, John Murphy from Missouri, and me, from near the end of the local bus line. Hurdlers, who also worked out in the fall, included John Smith from Illinois and Bob McDavid from Mississippi.

John Smith was also the team captain for the 1947 team. John started at Notre Dame before the war, but entered the Army Air Corp following Pearl Harbor. He became a bomber pilot based in Italy, flying missions over Europe in B-24 Liberators. He was a true war hero. I remember one of my first meetings with John. My buddy and teammate/classmate, Jim Miller, and I were going to practice one day, when John stopped us outside the field house. He gave us the once-over, and told us that our shoes needed shining. I didn't tell him that those were the only shoes I had. He didn't say anything about the rest of our attire, and I'm sure he could have. Jim (the team's pole-vaulter), the rest of the team, and I held John in high esteem. While at Notre Dame, he set hurdle records that weren't broken until a John Smith-coached Bill Fleming broke them while at Notre Dame. Fleming was a stalwart on the team and a nationally known hurdler.

Fall track participants became close over time, since we were in the same events. The only other freshman in the group was Paul Schwetshenau. For whatever reason, there were three in the group that I have maintained constant contact with over the years, right up to the present: Ernie McCullough, Bob McDavid, and Paul

Schwetshenau. It is unusual to keep in touch with anyone for 60 years. Our bonds had to be strong.

These three were very different, even on the track team. Ernie ran the 220, 440, and mile relay, earning three monograms. He was team captain in 1948 and ran in the 1948 Olympics on the Canadian team. He graduated magna cum laude after playing the violin in the Notre Dame Symphonette and serving as president of the Wranglers, a prestigious discussion group. I had the privilege of meeting his parents, when they came to visit us in our home on one of their trips to Notre Dame. After graduation, Ernie got his doctorate and went on to become a professor of Medieval Philosophy. He has such a mastery of the English language that reading his correspondence is a challenge to me. I look forward to his letters.

"Hey, Happy Smith!" Whenever I heard that, it had to be Robert Finley McDavid from McComb, Mississippi. (You know where that is, don't you?) I was not one to brim over with outward enthusiasm and had a tendency to see the glass as half empty instead of half full. I attributed that to having two dour grandfathers, both of whom had a hard life. Anyhow, Bob picked up on that, and I'm still "Happy Smith" to him.

Bob was a good hurdler, but lacked sprinter speed. That wasn't good, considering the level of competition Notre Dame faced. His other problem was that he was number two on his own team, because team mate Bill Fleming was one of the best in the country. Bob had to beat the other team's number one man to finish second. If it bothered him, it didn't show. He was always upbeat. Bob's best race should have been the 440 hurdles, but that event wasn't run much when Bob was in school. He still won three monograms and was always popular with the other athletes. After graduation, he got a doctorate, and spent his career as a professor of physical education at Indiana State University. While there, he devised an exercise system for Larry Bird. Today whenever the phone rings and "Happy Smith" is requested, I know it's R. Finley McDavid, ready to make my day.

Of the three, Paul Schwetshenau had the most in common with me. "Swets" was from Cincinnati, Ohio - then and now. We were both P.E. majors and had many of our classes together. In fact, we had all of our non-elective classes together. After our classes were over, we were at practice together, then supper together. Paul was strictly a quarter miler and won three monograms running the 440 and mile relay. Paul was the type of runner that is indispensable to the success of any team. More often than not, his contributions went unsung, except by those in the know. When Paul and I had nothing else to do, we would debate the merits of the Cubs and Cincinnati Reds. There was really nothing to debate. Paul went on to work as a financial analyst for General Electric.

Swets, Steve Provost, Ray Sobota, and I were of close or equal ability, a nice problem for Doc to have, since quarter milers are the backbone of any team. However, it was hard on those vying for relay spots. There was one run-off we all remember. Doc wanted Paul, Ray, and me to run a 440 trial - in snow flurries. Luckily, there wasn't any snow accumulation on the track yet, but it would have been a better story if there had.

The assistant coach during 1947 and 1948 was Bob Lawrence. Bob was another athlete who was at Notre Dame before Pearl Harbor, winning monograms in 1938, 1939, and 1940 as a hurdler. Bob didn't take defeats as calmly as Doc, especially when less than all-out effort was involved. No coach likes that.

One incident that everyone remembers with amusement happened at the Drake Relays. In one relay, Ray Sobota was running anchor when Notre Dame dropped the baton early in the race. By the time Ray got the baton, Notre Dame was hopelessly out of the race, so Ray didn't pour it on. The one runner who was still behind him started to close the gap but was not successful in overtaking him. Later in the day when we were all up in our hotel room, Coach Lawrence cornered Sobota. The rest of us were behind Coach and could see Sobota. By the time Coach got going, all of us behind Lawrence had a hard time to keep from breaking up.

Coach to Sobota: "Do you know who picked up on you? NORTHWESTERN!" Ray didn't know what to do - it was all he could do to keep a straight face. In fact, he couldn't, and neither could the rest of us.

Bob Lawrence was the kind of coach we needed to go along with Doc. Doc was laid back, but Bob kept us on our toes when we needed it. He'd been a navy officer during the war. Bob spent many hours with me on my start, and he was much appreciated.

Practice

Track practice was held every afternoon, on Cartier Field, which was located just north of the stadium. Later, Cartier Field was replaced by the new library. In the fall, the distance runners ran cross country and had a competitive schedule. Usually they practiced around the lakes and the golf course. The rest of us ran fall track in Cartier Field under the direction of the assistant track coach. This was a conditioning program, and we ran outside until it got too cold. Then we moved into the field house and ran indoors until it was warm enough to move outdoors.

While we were at fall practice, we had the opportunity to watch the football team practice. During the period when I was in school, the football team never lost a game. This was the period from 1946 through 1949, when the team had a 39-game winning streak. They were national champions two years during this time. Every Wednesday the team would scrimmage, and the ground shook during these scrimmages. Some of the scrimmages were better than the games on Saturday.

I really didn't know what to expect during my freshman year, and as it turned out, most of the season was spent finding out what I could do. The advantage was that as a freshman, no one really expected too much from me. In high school, my best time in the 100 yard dash was :10.6, terrible by today's standards. It wouldn't get me out of the qualifying rounds of a big meet. Back then, there just weren't any good sprinters in the area, and I was able to place well with that time. My best 220 time, :23.5, wasn't any better. The year spent in the navy following high school really helped. I was able to grow, adding size and strength, which paid off for me when I got to Notre Dame.

As the season progressed and I scored more and more points, I became more and more valuable to the team. Against Iowa, I placed third in the 60. In a dual meet with Michigan State, I finished second in the 60 yard dash. In the Big State meet, I took a third in the 100 and a second in the 220 behind Chuck Peters, the Big Ten champion from Indiana University. This was an exciting finish for the freshman from South Bend, and Doc Handy was pleased, but there was more to come.

The highlight of my freshman year came in Peoria, Illinois, where we had gone for a triangular meet with Bradley and Marquette. It was a nice sunny day, and a good-sized crowd turned out for the meet. I was nice and loose, and my feeling of pre-race nervousness was higher than usual. The only race I ran that day was the 100, and I led it all the way, finishing with a time of ten seconds flat. Ten flat (:10.0) was a benchmark time in the 100. If you couldn't run that, then you really couldn't call yourself a sprinter. I was elated with the time, and more importantly, with how well the race went. Not only did I win, but I also beat a sprinter from Marquette who had beaten me in the Conference finals in high school. I knew that a 10 flat time was not nearly good enough to get me very far in the competitive world where Notre Dame ran. This was a case of doing well, being happy with it, yet knowing I would have to improve. I knew that there were runners that I could never defeat, no matter how hard I worked and tried. Still, a sense of satisfaction ensues when you run a creditable time after working very hard, even though it may not be a world-class time.

Much of my freshman year was spent determining my best distances, and it soon became apparent what they were. The 60 yard dash, which is the indoor sprint, was too short for me. My best time was 6.3 in the 60, and that time would win a few races, depending on the opposition. It wouldn't beat the good competitors, however. The only person I couldn't beat in the sprints was Dave Murphy. The regular quarter milers could still beat me, but I had enough confidence now to think I could beat them, too. As an added incentive, relay teams usually went to the big meets when an individual would not, and most relay teams needed quarter milers. The Kansas and Drake Relays, two of the largest in the country, featured relays we ran. I didn't displace anyone on a relay team as a freshman, but during the next three years I had a place on the mile relay that hit the big meets.

My best distance was between 200 and 300 yards. The 440 was a little too far for me, but I trained for it and ran it in the mile relay, which did not change the fact that running the quarter (440) was a painful experience for me. The fact that I didn't have much stamina at that distance prevented me from training hard enough to really get my time down. My best time in the quarter was 49.0, which was run in the mile relay when Notre Dame finished third in the Drake Relays, running 3:18. That was a time and place finish that pleased all of us, since Drake was – and still is – one of the best meets in the country. Our season usually ended with the Central Collegiate Conference meet, held in Milwaukee the first week of June. Top athletes from all over the Midwest ran in this meet, as they used it as a tune-up for the NCAA meet the next week. As a freshman I was able to finish fourth in the 100, and ran on the 440 yard relay team that also finished fourth.

Doc Handy and Bob Smith *Photo Courtesy of University of Notre Dame*

I was able to win a monogram my freshman year, which exceeded my expectations. Doc Handy was pleased with my first season, and we both looked forward to my sophomore year.

5

The Olympic Trials

The medals aren't the important thing. The glory is nice, but it doesn't last. It's all about performing well and feeling deeply about it.

Daley Thompson, Decathlete, Olympic Gold Medalist

1948 and 1949

My sophomore and junior years were the high points of my track career, when most of my quality wins took place. We returned to Bradley for a triangular meet with Bradley and Drake. The year before, I had won the 100 with a time of ten flat (10.0), a breakthrough for me. My sophomore year, 1948, produced another breakthrough. The day was almost perfect, and so was my race. My time was 9.6 seconds, which tied the Notre Dame record and set a Bradley Field record. It was enough to bring Lee Daniel out of his living room. In the same meet, I won the 220 in 21.5 seconds, which was also a Bradley Field record.

A couple weeks later at home, Notre Dame was defeated in a dual meet by Michigan State. Although the team lost, it was another great day for me. I won the 100 in :09.8, which gave credence to my earlier :09.6 and set a Notre Dame school record for the 220 yard dash with a :21.1. This was run on a straightaway which isn't run anymore, so the record still stands. Shortly after, the 220 was run on a turn and the times and distances were switched to metric. It became the 200 meter dash. I had the pleasure of

44

coaching at Notre Dame when Bill Hurd broke all my records, with the exception of this one.

1948 was an Olympic year, with the games being held in London, England. The American team was chosen from those who placed in either the NCAA or National AAU meet. The National AAU meet was held at Marquette University in Milwaukee, Wisconsin, on July 2-3, and the NCAA meet was held on June 18-19, 1948 at the University of Minnesota at Minneapolis. The final Olympic Trials were held at Northwestern University in Evanston, Illinois, on July 9-10, 1948.

The time came for the team that would be going to the NCAA meet to be listed. Listed were Fleming, Kenny, Kittell, Leonard, McCullough, and Jim Murphy. I just assumed, based on the year I'd had so far, that I would be going to the NCAA meet, and was quite disappointed when my name wasn't listed. I thought Doc had his reasons, and it wasn't up to me to question him. Bill Fleming, however, saw the list and was quite upset that I wasn't going. He wanted me to talk with Doc. Again, I was reluctant to question the coach.

"OK," replied Bill, "I'll go talk with Doc."

And he did. Evidently, Doc had to send in the entries before I had posted my good times and didn't add me later. Doc then entered me, and I was very appreciative to Bill for what he had done. The lesson for me was to be more aggressive when the situation warranted, and speak up when I should. Old habits were hard to break, but I worked on it.

Because of Bill Fleming, I made the trip to Minneapolis. Events did not move smoothly. I was quickly eliminated in the 100 meter dash. The 200-meter dash went better. There were seven in my heat, where three were to qualify for the final. It appeared that Don Anderson of California and I had tied for third in the heat, and that finish was announced. The officials of the meet used a photo-timer, which took each runner's picture as they finished the race. When the results of the photo-timer were examined, it showed that I had nosed out Anderson and would be advancing to the finals. Who knows how it would have turned out if not for the photo-timer.

Photo-timer picture: First place Charlie Peters, Indiana University, second place Charley Parker, Texas, Third (top of picture) Don Anderson, California was nosed out by (bottom of picture) Bob Smith, Notre Dame *Photo courtesy of the NCAA*

There I was in the finals of the 200 meter dash in a race for the Olympics. If it hadn't been for Bill Fleming, I wouldn't have been there at all. If it weren't for the photo-timer, I might not have advanced to the finals. There were nine in the finals with the first six advancing to the Olympic trials at Northwestern. I finished sixth in the finals of the NCAA 200 meters, and so advanced. This had a grim reality, however, as realistically my chances of placing in the top three were slim and none. In track, it is easy to compare times. Major upsets at this level are rare, but they do happen, and one should hope and train for the best.

The Olympic trials were held in July, which meant having to practice and maintain my conditioning alone for a month. This challenge was something entirely new to me, and believe it or not, it was difficult to do. Two others on our team qualified for the finals: Bill Leonard in the 1500 meters, and Jim Kittell in the steeplechase. Neither of them could be any help to me with my training, since they trained at different distances. All of this happened when I was fatigued by the long season we had just finished, and here I had to practice for a month all by myself in the summer heat.

Olympic Trials: Bob Smith, Bill Leonard, and Jim Kittell. *Photo Courtesy of University of Notre Dame*

The day of the Olympic trials was oppressively hot. I didn't wear our heavy blue warm-ups, instead wearing the lighter gray sweat suit we wore in practice, just like back at Central High School. This time it was by choice. When the meet started and the 200-meter race was called up, I was in the second heat with three to qualify. I was in lane four. The lane assignment couldn't have been better. When the race started, before I even made it to the curve, a red blur went by me in lane three. The red blur was Mel Patton from Southern California, who not only won the Olympic trials, but was also the eventual winner of the race in the Olympics. Others in my age group, which included long time nemeses Paul Bienz and Chuck Peters, didn't make it either. I had to console myself with the fact I was the sixth fastest college runner at 200 meters in the country. Despite this, my dreams were coming true.

The satisfaction for me came in knowing I spent the day with world-class athletes, and, although I had no chance of winning, I was there. Hard work and persistence paid off. Someone else was sitting on the end of the bench.

Ernie McCullough, captain of the 1948 team, was Canadian. He qualified for the Olympics with the Canadian team and went to

London. He didn't place at the Olympics, but we were all happy for Ernie. Being able to run in the London Olympics was a great experience for him.

After the Olympics

Once the Olympic trials were over, my season was finally over, and I reported to my summer job at the Post Office. One day out on the route, I had just finished putting mail in the box on the porch when a little dog pushed the screen door open and came out yapping at me and wagging its tail. I thought that was a good sign, so I went down the porch steps and headed down the sidewalk. The dog then ran down the steps and bit me. Every day after that, the owner of the dog would tell me "He ain't sick yet," as though the dog would catch something from *me*. My summer vacation flew by, and before I knew it the time had come to start my junior year.

6

The Climax

My strategy is simple. I get out in front early – run as hard as I can – for as long as I can.

Steve Ovett, Distance Runner, Olympic Gold Medalist

As a junior, I began thinking of graduation. I was enjoying my classes and doing well. It was time to get together with my academic advisor to make sure I had scheduled the right courses and had the right number of hours to graduate. All was well on the academic front, and I was on a clear course to graduate.

There were some exciting changes in track that year. Our new assistant coach, John Smith, had been the 1947 captain. John was assisting Doc while finishing his law degree. The members of the team received his appointment with joy. The previous spring, Bill Leonard had been elected captain. This was a popular choice, since Bill was held in high esteem among his peers.

I think every relay runner has one race that stands out in his memory, one that has never been forgotten no matter how many years have passed. For me, that was the mile relay at the 1949 Michigan AAU indoor meet at Ann Arbor. This relay was a special matched race, with Michigan, Michigan State, and Notre Dame the only entrants. Michigan was anchored by 800 meter Olympian

Herb Barten, Michigan State by Jack Dianetti, an outstanding quarter miler and middle distance man, and Notre Dame by me. This race was the last race of the meet, and the sizable crowd (for an indoor meet) was getting noisy. Notre Dame got off to a good start, and the first three Notre Dame runners (Provost, Schwetshenau, and Sobota) each ran outstanding quarters. By the time I got the baton, they had staked me to a seven or eight yard lead. Now, all I had to do was to hold off two of the best around for a quarter and the gold medals were ours. I put out everything I had, and did manage to hold them off to win. Let me say, however, that if there had been another two or three yards to go, I would have been third. After the race, I went into the locker room and had dry heaves. That race hurt physically, but it was satisfying emotionally. The 440 was a trifle too far for me, but the pain was always worth it.

The next meet was one I had been looking forward to – the Michigan State Relays, which offered the 300 yard dash. I was at my best at that distance. I won the 300 at the Michigan State Relays with a time of :31.6. At the indoor Central Collegiate Conference meet at Michigan State, I won with a time of :31.4, which at the time was a meet record and tied the field house record. I wished that there were more races at 300 yards. My competitors at that distance were those I faced in the sprints and quarter, and for many of them 300 was a trifle too long, and for others it was a trifle too short. For me it was just right.

We took an unusual trip in 1949 to the Southern Relays at Birmingham, Alabama, which involved a long train trip both ways. The day of the meet was cold and blustery. My nemesis, Paul Bienz, was there to win the 100, and a sprinter named Neely from Mississippi State sneaked into second, while I had to settle for third. We ran the 880 relay that day and placed second. All in all, the Irish have had better days. The only southern hospitality we encountered was at a party the night after the meet given by the meet committee. The party had girls and everything. (It would be another twenty years before Notre Dame went coed.) We also had the opportunity to meet some of our opponents. On balance, though, most of us were more than ready to catch the train back home.

1949 Michigan State Relays, 300 yd dash finals. Bob Smith, Bob Schepers, MSC, Irving Petross, Wayne State, and Harry Cogswell, OSU. Photo was taken at Michigan State, Jenison Fieldhouse. *Photo courtesy of University of Notre Dame*

The Drake Relays were an infamous low point that year. Bill Leonard and I dropped the baton on our exchange in the sprint medley with disastrous results. Notre Dame was effectively out of the race. It isn't every day you drop the baton in front of 25,000 people, but it happens.

In the sprint medley (440-220-220-880) a team is really no better than the half miler. By the time the drop was made, Bill was already behind some of the best half milers in the Midwest, so it was questionable how we would have fared without the drop. The first three runners on the relay team hadn't given Bill much support. The dropped baton just finished a bad effort against top competition. Although Bill Leonard was primarily a miler and half miler, he possessed enough speed to run on the mile relay. Without that speed, he wouldn't have so done so well in the distances. Bill and I ran together, both on the mile relay and on the sprint medley relay when we were at the Drake Relays.

Our last regular season meet was the Central Collegiate Conference meet held in Milwaukee. Previously, I had done reasonably well in this meet, but in '49 I had a great meet. I finished third in the 100, which was a fast field that year. The winning time was :09.6, with the entire field finishing within a couple of yards. I was timed with a :09.8 by one our team members, and :09.7 by another. Back then, only the winner was timed officially.

The race with the greatest crowd interest was the 220, which featured Ed Tunnicliff, one of the heroes in Northwestern's football victory in the Rose Bowl played the previous January. Tunnicliff was also a good trackman. Somehow, being the football player made him the favorite in the 220, but that night he finished second to Smith of Notre Dame. It was one of my best races around a turn, and I led all the way. The track wasn't in top condition, because it had been soaked by heavy rains the night before and earlier that day. My winning time in the 220 was :21.8, which was two tenths off my fastest time around a curve.

Team Travel

One aspect of team sports that one doesn't think about is team travel: getting to wherever the competition was to take place. Getting to the meets was a big adventure, some trips more than others. Traveling to certain meets created indelible memories that became part of the total experience.

The Notre Dame track team traveled by bus, train, or a combination of the two. The Wright Brothers' invention was never utilized during the time that I was there. Trips to Purdue were always by bus, as were trips to Chicago, Indianapolis, and Bloomington.

The bus also took us to East Lansing, Michigan, whenever we had meets at Michigan State. You would think there would be nothing unusual about taking the bus to East Lansing, until you realize that two out of the three trips each season took place during the winter. Interstate highways had not yet been built, and the road to East Lansing was a two-lane highway. More often than not, there was a snowstorm (or so it seemed), and one memorable trip was taken during an ice storm. Not only did we slip and slide all the way up there, but we arrived too late to run in the qualifying heats. A few of the athletes missed their events. I was afraid during the entire trip.

Depending on the meet time schedule, sometimes we would stay overnight. Some trips would be made in one day, which would be a strain and a drain. Whenever possible, Doc would stop at Win Schuler's Restaurant in Marshall, Michigan, on the way up and order dinner for the trip home. Now, a steak dinner at Win Schuler's was something not easily forgotten (and they haven't been), but somehow eating it at midnight following a day of strenuous competition detracted from it somewhat for me.

Special Memories

My most memorable trip was the trip to Columbia, Missouri, to compete against the University of Missouri. On a

Friday evening, the team took the South Shore Railroad, an electric commuter train, to Chicago. Once in Chicago, we transferred to a train with sleeping cars, and we spent the night on the train as it took us to St. Louis. When we got to St. Louis the next morning, we only had a short wait until we boarded another train that dumped us in the middle of nowhere. We just sat by the tracks and waited. Shortly, a local train came chugging along, and we all piled on board. The car had a potbellied stove at one end. Luckily, it wasn't needed. It seemed as though that train stopped every 15 minutes or so. At one stop, a little old lady carrying a basket got on. The basket was covered with what looked like a checked towel, and a chicken was allowed to stick its head out of the basket.

The trip into Columbia was soon finished, and we had to go straight to the track for the meet. This time the news was better, as we defeated a fine Missouri team 67 to 64. Following the meet we headed for home, reversing the way we came, although as I remember it, this time we were able to take a train straight to St. Louis.

Once we went to Penn State at State College, Pennsylvania. We started the trip by taking a bus to Plymouth, Indiana, about 24 miles south of South Bend. Then we caught a train to Pittsburgh, where we spent the night. The next morning we took another train to Altoona, where we transferred to a bus that took us to Penn State. We didn't have much time to rest before meet time. Not surprisingly, we lost the meet, 69 to 62. I lost both sprints to their fine sprinter, Wilbert Lancaster. This was not surprising, since he had beaten me in the 60 when Penn State was at Notre Dame the year before. Right after the meet we boarded the bus that took us to the train in Pittsburgh. A train to Plymouth and another bus to Notre Dame completed the trip.

The University of Pittsburgh was on our schedule in 1950, and we had a meet with them at Pitt. By this time, we knew the way, and the time schedule was such that we weren't rushed before the meet. It was a cold, raw, windy day, and we lost the meet by one third of a point. I think we were all glad to get back to our homework.

Our other trips were uneventful, but they afforded the team a chance to get to know each other better, and on some trips a person could even study!

The Longest Trip

The NCAA meet in 1949 was held in the Los Angeles Coliseum. Whether to send us to the meet was debated by the Athletic Department Administration, which included the athletic director, Moose Krause, and the business manager, Herb Jones. They didn't want to spend the money to send us unless we could guarantee that we would place. Now Moose, of all people, should have known that it was impossible to guarantee the outcome. The chances of my placing in that particular meet were almost nonexistent, and I'm not being negative or defeatist here. Throughout the country there were at least a dozen athletes with times appreciably faster than mine, and they would all be in L.A., so we couldn't guarantee anything. This time Doc went to bat for us. I don't know what he said to them, but they agreed that Bill Fleming, John Helwig, and I could go to the meet in Los Angeles. Actually, we thought that Doc wanted to go to the meet, too.

We did go to the meet. We took the train there and back, and while there, we didn't place in any of the events we entered. We did enjoy the train trip, as we spent time together and with Doc. I imagine that the Athletic Department wished they had their decision (and money) back. All of us, which I imagine included Doc, felt that we had earned the trip, regardless of whether we placed or not. It was a positive for the program and let others know that Notre Dame valued its track program and those who achieved in it. We felt that our presence at the meet was an incentive for other athletes to attend Notre Dame.

Ending with Joy

The only thing remaining in the season was the annual team dinner, which was held at the Sunny Italy Restaurant in South

Bend. Two items of business were to make the monogram awards and to elect the next year's captain.

The election made me very nervous, because I knew that I had a chance to win. The first ballot resulted in a tie, as did the second. Then during the third ballot, someone changed his vote, and I was elected captain. That was – and remains – one of the highlights of my life. History was being made there, because I was the only South Bend resident *ever* to be elected captain of a Notre Dame track team, and to my knowledge there has not been another. Words cannot describe my elation over this election, but I also realized that responsibility came along with the honor, and I resolved to do what it took to measure up. My senior year was ahead, and it was full of challenges.

7

Culmination of a Career

A smooth sea never made a skillful mariner.
US Senator, Hubert H. Humphrey

Senior Year Challenges

One of the biggest challenges I faced during my senior year was to maintain the level of achievement attained my sophomore and junior years. Those were my record-producing years; those were the years when I could run two or three races in a meet and produce good times in the process. I felt I had reached my physical peak by the end of my junior year. My senior year was my fourth year in the program. It was a rigorous program, indeed.

The season started in September with fall track, which was a general conditioning program that lasted until it became too cold to stay outside. We then moved inside and ran in the field house until it was warm enough to go back outside. While indoors, we went through the indoor meet schedule. When spring finally came, we went back outside and proceeded through the outdoor schedule, which lasted until June.

Practice was usually held at least six days a week and varied according to the time of season. During the season, Monday was "over distance day." Quarter milers (440) would usually run at least one 660. Since the quarter mile was too far for me to begin with, the 660 was really tough for me. Tuesday we did speed work, and the quarter milers ran 330s and possibly 220s. Wednesday was usually starting practice and more speed work. Thursday we worked on passing the baton, along with more starts. Friday was a tapering-off day, with our thoughts on the Saturday meet. Friday also might be a traveling day for away meets.

As I got into my senior year, staying sharp became a real problem for me, since I didn't possess great natural stamina. More recovery time was needed to produce the same results. Friday was a light warm-up day when we were home, and eventually I needed to take Friday off entirely to produce a winning time on Saturday. Later in my senior year, I needed two days for a complete recovery.

Sprinters are, by nature, nervous and high-strung. They have to be, since the short sprints (I include everything up through the 440 here) are run with a lot of nervous energy and adrenaline flow. Not only is there physical preparation for a meet, but there is mental preparation as well. I would start getting "hyped" about Thursday, depending on the meet and competition. On race day, right before the race, I would get ready mentally to focus on the race specifically. If someone had come up behind me right before a race and said "boo," I would have jumped at least a foot. The running of a race not only uses physical energy but mental energy as well. All of this is takes its toll over time. It takes work to maintain physical and mental conditioning.

Socially Challenged

During my years at Notre Dame, my social life had been virtually non-existent. Track and my studies consumed practically all of my time. I wanted to do well in the classroom, and I had to keep my grades up to stay on the team. I also wanted to do well on the track. Weekends spent on campus usually involved making up work – usually lab work – that had been missed during track trips. Vacations were spent either writing term papers or doing whatever jobs I could find to produce income. Passing in the classroom was 70%, although an average of 77% was necessary to be eligible and to graduate. I would graduate cum laude with an average of 88.8%, which represented a lot of time and effort.

You might think that because I was a Physical Education major, I spent most of my time in the gym. Not so. When I graduated, I had 146 semester hours of credit, with only 19 hours spent in the gym or in outdoor activities. That meant I spent 126 hours in the classroom in a rigorous academic curriculum, more than the 120-hour normal class load over four years. As a result, there wasn't much time for social life. I might add there wasn't much means, either.

In October of my senior year, a very important event occurred. My teammate/classmate Jim Miller asked me to go to a party with him in Mishawaka on a Saturday night. My response was pretty predictable: "No – why would I want to go to a party? I have things to do."

Miller persisted, and I finally agreed to go with him. To say I was glad I went would be an understatement. During the evening, I circulated among those there, and suddenly, *"there she was!"*

"She" was Candida Sarkisian, who lived in Mishawaka and had graduated from Mishawaka High School in 1945, the year I graduated from Central. We were married the following September. To understand the significance of this, you have to understand the rivalry between Mishawaka and Central. In 2007, we will have been married 57 years.

My Last Season

John Smith finished law school and had moved on. Our new assistant coach was Bill Leeds, a journalism student. Bill didn't have much track experience, and he had to work with a team loaded with seniors who thought they knew everything. Everyone knew his limitations, but everyone cooperated with Bill. I feel he enjoyed his time with us.

The first indoor meet of the 1950 season was the Michigan State Relays. After that meet, we had an unusual quirk in our schedule: three dual home meets in a row. On successive Saturdays we defeated Missouri, Purdue, and Indiana. Each meet had a good student turnout to support the team, and we didn't disappoint.

Against Missouri the score was 66½-47½. I lost the 60 in a very close finish, but ran on the winning mile relay team. Our team felt good about this particular meet, because Missouri was a very tough competitor. Whenever we could beat the Tigers, it meant we'd had a good day.

Against Purdue, we won 64½-49½. For the second week in a row, I was beaten in the 60, this time by Harold Omer of the Boilermakers. For the second week in a row, the winning time was :06.3. I matched the time, but was nosed out. Purdue's fine mile relay defeated Notre Dame, but by the time of the relay, the Irish had the meet wrapped up. As of that date, Purdue had never beaten Notre Dame in a dual meet.

Our third win of the month came against the Indiana Hoosiers, 63-51. Indiana University still had Chuck Peters in the sprints. Doc conceded the 60 to Peters, but he put me in the 60 anyway. The very next event was the 440, and Doc entered me in that race, also. The 60 produced my third loss of the month in the 60, only this time Indiana produced a one-two finish and I finished third. After the 60, I walked from the finish line back to the starting line, turned my starting blocks around, and got ready to immediately run the quarter. Doc knew what he was doing, as Indiana proved weak in the quarter. Teammate Bob Boyne and I tied for first and Indiana was third. Our winning time was :51.6, a mediocre time for that distance. Although Doc gave me the afternoon off from the mile relay, the Irish won that race easily.

Although I was 0-3 for the month in the 60, I knew I had done the best I could, and two of the three losses were very close. Only the race with Peters wasn't close. I did have a first (tie) in the 440, and a mile relay win against Missouri, so the month wasn't a total loss.

Getting in condition to run the 440 was a good idea. Quarter milers are the backbone of any team. No team can have too many. Good quarter milers can be dropped down to the 220, pushed up to the 600 or 880, or be converted into low hurdlers. The Indiana dual was an example of how I could contribute even though I was beaten in the 60. The 440 was available, and we were able to tie for first, giving us 8 points instead of only 5. (In dual meets, points are 5-3-1.) I have never regretted running the 440 as well as the sprints, but I never ran an all-out 440 (the only way to do it) without paying the price in pain.

The Chicago Daily News Relays was one of the first meets to be televised. The meet was on a Chicago station, so the reception in South Bend was pretty snowy, although the telecast was watchable. This meet was interesting because it was run on a board track, 11 laps to the mile with two rather steeply banked turns. The track had a little bounce to it, and special shoes with little pin spikes had to be worn. Racing on this track required skill and racing strategy. Whoever got to the turn first could, with skill, pretty much control the inside and effectively force the others to the outside, making them run farther. I had no experience on boards, nor did the others in our foursome, so we had problems. We did the best we could, finished third, and enjoyed the new experience.

Indoor tracks vary in composition and length. Some are banked, some unbanked. The old field house at Notre Dame was a clay 220 banked track. The track in the old Jenison Field House at Michigan State was a clay 220 unbanked track. The track at Purdue was a clay unbanked track. The variations made it difficult to have official track and meet records.

When Notre Dame built the Joyce Center in 1969, it had a composition 176 yard unbanked track. This was not a good situation, since it had eight lanes. For races run in lanes all the way (for example the 440 and 600), the runners in the outside lane had an advantage because they ran one turn less than the runner in lane one. Running a turn, especially on a short track, is always more difficult because the inside lane is sharper. The track in Notre Dame's new Loftus Center is 352 yards with a composition surface, which makes it one of the finest indoor facilities anywhere.

Jim Kittell, Paul Schwetshenau, and Ray Espenan. *Photo Courtesy of Paul Schwetshenau*

Tragedy struck the football and track teams during the spring, when Ray Espenan died as a result of an accident on a trampoline. Ray, a broad (long) jumper on the track team, was a senior in the Physical Education school. He was student teaching at Central High School. He was demonstrating the use of the trampoline when he came down wrong, breaking his neck.

Ray lived about two weeks before he died. It was my responsibility as team captain to determine what the team should do for Ray. After polling the team, it was decided to have masses said in his memory, which was done. Several years later, a gifted pole-vaulter from Riley High School in South Bend, Bob Gordes, died as a result of a similar accident, so I have known two athletes who knew what they were doing and yet died on a trampoline. You don't have to guess my feelings on the use of the trampoline in our schools – or anywhere else, for that matter.

Going into the last month of the season, we had two meets at home. The first was a dual meet with the Spartans of Michigan State. The dual with the Spartans turned out the same as all of the other meets with them during my four years at Notre Dame. Our team failed to beat them, but I had good luck individually. I had set the Notre Dame school record of :21.1 in the 220 against them earlier. In our final meet, I was able to win both the 100 and the 220 with times of :10.1 and :21.6 on what was a slow track. The 220 was especially gratifying because the Spartans put their ace hurdler, Horace Smith, in especially to beat me. Earlier in the meet, Horace had nosed out Bill Fleming in the high hurdles in the record time of :14.3. Beating Horace Smith was not easy. I think most of us were glad to be saying goodbye to the "green shirts" for the year. In the years immediately after World War II, Michigan State's track program was outstanding. Arguably, those teams were the best in the history of the school, and it was no disgrace losing to them. In fact, I believe we were the better for running them those four years.

The last home meet was the Closed Central Collegiate Conference meet. Only schools that were members of the Central Collegiate Conference could participate. Those schools were Notre Dame, Marquette, Bradley, Drake, DePaul, Loyola, and Butler. Michigan State was a member, but chose not to run in this meet. The Open Central Collegiate Conference meet was open to any school and had been held at Marquette Stadium in Milwaukee in early June. The Open meet was one of the major meets in the Midwest, and the top athletes used it as a warm-up for the NCAA meet.

I was disappointed in the outcome of the Closed meet as far as my finishes were concerned, since I finished third in the 100 behind Don Pettie of Drake and Charles Whittingham of Loyola. I had beaten Pettie before in this event. Don and I took turns beating each other over the years. I guess 1950 was his turn. I had better luck in the 220, managing to win with a slow time of :22. Notre Dame won the over-all meet with 89 points to runner-up Marquette's 50.

My Last Meet

My last meet for Notre Dame, the Open Centrals at Milwaukee, turned out to be one of the low points of my whole career. The year before I had finished third in the 100 and scored an upset win in the 220. This had been one of my major wins. In 1950 I failed to qualify for the finals in either the 100 or the 220. The Open Centrals were held the Saturday following graduation at Notre Dame. It wasn't easy working out after school was out, graduation was over, and the summer heat was upon us. Perhaps these factors contributed to my poor showing in the meet.

Going into the meet, I was bone weary, and three days of rest hadn't restored the old zip. Not only was I physically tired, but mentally tired as well. That particular meet was no time to have an off day, tired or not. I had to go back to my freshman year to find a meet where I didn't place where I had expected.

This last disappointment was a combination of factors and needed to be put behind me. "As one door is closed, another is opened," and it was time to move on. In the first race I ever ran in high school, when Coach Anson had to pick me up off the track, I had been disappointed in the result. Fast forward to the last race of my career at Notre Dame when I failed to qualify at the Centrals, I would have to say that I was disappointed in that result, too. In the span of time between these two disappointments, I had a terrific career: four monograms, records in the 100, 220, and 300, and the honor of being the only South Bend native ever to be elected captain. There were many memories formed during those years that are still tucked in the crannies of my brain. My teammates and coaches – especially Doc Handy – all occupy a special place in my heart.

Jim Miller, Bob Smith, and Pete Varda at graduation.
Photo Courtesy of Paul Schwetshenau

Part II
Coaching Track and Field

The coach's job is to prepare the athlete to win. To prepare the athlete physically and psychologically to compete. Once the athlete gets to the starting line, he's on his own.

Author unknown

Coaching is a challenging "next step" for an athlete. It reveals a whole different side of the sport. The competition of athlete against athlete is raised to a whole new level, as coach competes against coach, team against team. The coach focuses on strategies that maximize individual potential while maximizing team performance. It is a rewarding arena where lives can be changed.

While this book focuses on events and teams in South Bend, Indiana, the location could be Anywhere, USA. The challenges and achievements are the same, only the names and the dates change.

8
The Dawn of a Coaching Career

To venture into the unknown, to search for your maximum potential, to achieve the impossible or highly improbably is life's greatest satisfaction. It takes intense preparation, total dedication and the risk of failure. If you have paid the price and give 100%, you're a winner.

Bob Gries, NFL Owner and Ultra Marathon Runner

Graduation and Employment

Gaining employment following graduation was on the mind of almost everyone in the Physical Education School, because most of us were looking for a teaching/coaching job, preferably in a high school. Schools (mostly Catholic) from all over the country would contact Notre Dame looking for coaches. Most jobs were for football coaches. None were for track only. Teaching job openings came from various sources: from the schools themselves, from agencies that were in the business of brokering teaching and coaching jobs, and from friends and relatives who provided leads.

During my job quest, I heard from Greybull, Wyoming with a position of 6-man football coach and track coach. I also heard from Omaha, Nebraska, Davenport, Iowa, and a military school in Florida. None of them offered a track/teaching offer. In the meantime, I applied in South Bend, my hometown. After an interview with Mr. Forrest Wood, South Bend's Director of Physical Education and Recreation, I was offered the position of teacher and head track coach at Riley High School on South Bend's south side. The teaching would be seventh grade science, which would be new for me, since I hadn't done student teaching in the classroom. It didn't take long for me to accept South Bend's offer. That marked the beginning of a lifetime career spent on the south side, and the former Central Bear became a Riley Wildcat.

Upon graduation from Notre Dame in June 1950, I started graduate school at Indiana University. I would get my Master's Degree from Indiana University by going summers at Bloomington and Saturday mornings at the Indiana Extension in South Bend. I completed my degree in 1953.

In September, 1950, I began my teaching and coaching career, being mindful of the examples set for me by my own grade and high school teachers, by Bert Anson, George Cooper, John Scannell, and Elvin (Doc) Handy. I would strive to measure up, because teaching is an awesome responsibility. I also got married, another awesome responsibility.

Coaching at Riley High School

The phone rang at 3 a.m., waking me from a sound sleep. It was the mother of one of my trackmen, telling me that he was still over at his girlfriend's house, he refused to listen to her, and he wouldn't come home. Could I go over to his girlfriend's house, get him, and bring him home? "He will listen to you," she said.

I must not have been able to think clearly, for I told her, "Okay, I'll be right over." This, mind you, was on a school night. I went to the student's home and got directions to the girl's house. I had barely gotten on her porch when the door opened a crack and the young man was there saying, "I'll be right with you, Coach." When I got him home, I left him with the message that I would deal with him later. Hopefully, "later" would afford me some time to figure out just how to deal with this.

I had been in contact with the mother earlier, because the boy had trouble passing his physical for track due to a possible heart problem, and she was also having some problems controlling him. I ended up talking with him and letting him know that under no circumstances was anything remotely resembling this episode ever to occur again. He knew I wasn't kidding, and I never had any more trouble with him. He went on to win the conference meet in the half mile, and finished fifth in the state meet in the half mile. Following graduation, he enlisted and served in the Marine Corps.

This is only one example of the challenges a coach faces in dealing with athletes.

– I received a good education at Notre Dame. During the fall semester of my senior year, I had a course covering the coaching of football and basketball, and during the spring semester, there was one covering track and baseball. The football and basketball course was taught by assistant coaches, and the track and baseball course by the head coaches. The legendary Jake Kline handled baseball, and, of course, Doc Handy taught track. Time in class was spent on the fundamentals of the sport and how to coach these fundamentals.

In Doc's case, he had all of us actually do the events. When he got to the pole vault, he had second thoughts about having me do it, since we were in the middle of the track season, and he knew what would be likely to happen if I actually tried to get off the ground. To no one's surprise, I was excused from the pole vault.

Unfortunately, the University did not prepare us to deal with problems like the one above. On any athletic team, there are always those who need guidance to help them through the tough teen years, and more often than not, it is the coach who provides it. A major part of coaching deals with the athletes, one on one, and helping them where it is both needed and wanted. It is something that the coach is in a position to do, and it takes experience, slowly acquired, if he is to be successful. It is something that usually has to be learned on the job, since it is something the colleges don't address as they should.

Most beginning coaches believe that all they have to do is coach, and that is very far from the truth. In most high schools, the coach is also the equipment manager, the trainer, and guidance counselor, at least as it relates to sports. The coach may be responsible for arranging transportation to the meets and for dealing with the dirty laundry. Of course, there will be at least one student manager to help, but the coach has to see to it that the student manager does the job. The coach has to plan practice, go over practice plans with his assistant coach (if there is one), then conduct practice.

I believe that track is one of the most difficult sports to coach, since it involves several widely different activities: teaching the fine points of pole vaulting, shot putting, high jumping, hurdling, and distance running to mention a few. It's a rare coach who is expert in all of these events to begin with, and even an experienced coach has some weaker events. Working with student athletes is only part of the coach's job. The coach usually teaches five classes a day with the attendant preparation for them. Those classes are the main reason the coach was hired in the first place. Relationships with other coaches are also important, and sometimes can cause problems of their own.

Coaching a spring sport presents its own challenges. Athletes that participate in other sports earlier in the school year often tire of sports and pass up track, simply because they are tired of the discipline and not ready for another sport. Competition for athletes among sports that share the same season can also be a problem. While I was at Riley, spring basketball coincided with track and baseball. Spring basketball practice could continue up until the State Finals. If the team lost in the first round, the sectional tournament, it could still practice the three weeks before the finals. Members of the basketball program who played baseball or ran track weren't allowed to leave basketball until the last possible date, even if they were needed in the spring sports and the time they were missing was an important conditioning period for track or baseball.

The football/baseball coach and the basketball coach were veteran coaches, pretty much set in their ways. Tact was not their strong suit, so every spring there was a hassle over a few athletes. The main argument was between the two veterans, but there were times when I was drawn into it. As a rookie, I tried to stay out of the fray.

What ultimately happened was that we developed our own group of track-only athletes. The growing success of the cross country program meant that more and more of the track athletes became involved in cross country

Another problem that a track coach at Riley had at that time was related to the facilities. The track was located behind the school. It was a quarter mile track with square turns. It was possible to run the one hundred yard dash and the high hurdles on a straightaway, but the 220 yard dash and the low hurdles had to be run around a turn which was almost square. The track was located next to the Studebaker Golf Course, and due to the lay of the land, sand continually eroded from the golf course onto the first curve of the track. Due to drainage problems, the second curve of the track resembled a water hazard more often than not, so we had sand problems on one curve and water problems on another. The jumping pits were nothing more than well-maintained sand pits. The broad jump (now long jump) pit wasn't bad, the high jump pit a little better, but the pole vault pit was a disaster. During the time I was coaching, we had one of the best pole-vaulters in the state, Dick Liechty, who finished second in the State in 1953. He achieved that in spite of his practice facilities. The baseball field was located in the infield of the track, and both practices took place at the same time. More than one trackman was hit by an errant baseball.

Team rules are a necessary but difficult challenge for a coach. My belief was that fewer rules were better, but they must be enforceable. I felt I was well equipped to address that issue, because I knew firsthand what it took to succeed. I expected all participants to do their very best, which meant that as growing and developing teenagers, they had to treat their bodies with respect. They could not subject themselves to any substance that would interfere with their top performance. Smoking and/or drinking were not allowed, and everyone understood that right from the start. The penalty was dismissal from the team for the remainder of the season.

The other rule dealt with attendance. The second unexcused absence from practice meant dismissal. I wanted to know when someone was not going to be there. I was quite lenient when it came to reasons for missing. After all, not many kids would go to the coach, give a far-out reason, and expect it to fly. I wanted each member of the team to develop a sense of responsibility and commitment. Combined with a hard work ethic and a good attitude, these qualities should ensure success, not just in track, but in life as well.

One of the hardest things I had to learn was that not all my athletes were willing to work as hard as I did. Most did, but not all. Inexperienced track athletes really don't realize how much work they can take, or how much potential they have, until they are pushed to the limit. Pushing that limit is the job of the coach as motivator.

The first year I coached at Riley, our conference meet was at Purdue, and our success was limited. My wife drove to see the meet, and afterward spoke to one of our distance men, Jim Lakatos, who had a disappointing race.

"That's okay, you'll do better the next time," she said.

His answer was, "That's not the half of it. Now I've got to ride back with old Simon."

He was referring to Simon Legree – me. Jim Lakatos went on to be the number one man on my first cross country team. Jim had run for my predecessor, Wayne Wakefield, who was a good coach but rather quiet and laid back.

Wayne was a basketball coach by trade, and took the Riley Wildcats to the final game of the state tourney in 1945. I'm sure I worked Jim harder than Wayne did.

Jim Lakatos

It's also possible that Jim had made up his mind to work harder and was ready to respond to my prodding. Once you can get an athlete to see the results of hard work, and others see the results, the coach's job is easier. Success breeds success.

Assistance from Assistants

I was fortunate enough to have an assistant coach. In my 8-year tenure at Riley, I had three assistants, and I was more than happy with each of them. Much of the success the team achieved wouldn't have happened without the contributions of the assistant coaches. Actually, in my mind they were not "assistants," but rather, "associates."

When I began, my associate was A.B. Meyer, a veteran math teacher and long-time coach who had been around the track many times. In fact, A.B. was old enough to be my father and was a very unflappable person, just the person to work with a "flappable" rookie coach.

Riley won the 1952 City Outdoor Meet, beating Central 54½ to 52⁵/₆. I give full credit for that win to A.B. Earlier in the spring, Riley beat Central in the City Indoor meet 52½ to 52, so the outdoor meet promised to be close. It was. The City Meet included Central, Riley, Washington, and John Adams. Each of these schools had good athletes. In the City Outdoor, the meet came down to the pole vault. Going into the pole vault, Central had a 3 point lead in the meet. Jack Cote of Central and Ed Willamowski of Riley tied for third in the vault, with Bill Forrest of Washington and Dick Liechty of Riley going for first. If Dick won, Riley would win the meet. If Bill won, Central would win. I could see that the pressure was building on the remaining vaulters, and that A.B. saw it too.

A.B. went over to talk with Liechty, gave him a few tips, and calmed him down. Dick made his first vault at 11'9", which Forrest equaled. The bar went up three more inches to 12', and A.B. gave Dick a couple more tips. Liechty made 12' on his first try, scraping the bar on the way down. The bar bounced and stayed. Forrest then missed all three attempts at 12'. Dick Liechty won the pole vault, Riley won the meet, and in Bob Smith's mind, A.B. Meyer won Coach of the Year. After the 1952 season, A.B. Meyer retired from coaching. He had done his job by giving the young head coach good advice.

Dick Liechty

Dick Liechty was hailed for winning that meet for Riley. But wait! The meet was really won in the long jump pit, where Riley picked up three very unexpected points. Jim Cherpes of Riley finished second to Cashaw of Washington but beat Jack Cote, who finished third for Central. Those three points gave Riley the points that Liechty needed to go with the pole vault points to win the meet. If Cherpes hadn't beaten Cote in the long jump, it wouldn't have mattered what Liechty did.

Let's take a look at the unlikely hero, Jim Cherpes, a senior on the Riley track team. He was on the team in 1951 and 1952. Jim was a hardworking young man who was very cooperative in everything we asked him to do. He had "bringing up," as the saying goes. His parents had an interest in him and attended the meets. Jim enjoyed running and the associations with his teammates. He did the best he could, which for the most part wasn't enough for tangible results. The problem, if there was one, was that he had limited ability. During the entire 1951 season he scored *one* varsity point: a third in the long jump against LaPorte. He worked hard and tried hard. Although he was never quite good enough to place, he didn't give up.

During the 1952 season, Jim's strong work ethic continued but there wasn't much improvement. He never gave up, however. He finished third in the 880 against Culver Military for one point.

77

Going into the season finale, the City Meet, he had a total of one varsity point for the entire season, two in his entire career. He was entered in the long jump and had the best day of his career. Everything fell into place, and he got off the best long jump he had ever made, finishing second, and scoring three vital points. With that one jump of 20 feet, he scored more points in one meet than he had scored over two full years of effort. Not only that, but his effort provided the winning edge for his team. This is an example of what can happen if an athlete doesn't give up.

The importance of Jim's success in the City Meet escaped the media, and I'm not sure whether Jim fully realized it at the time, but his coach did. I was very proud of him. It is also the coach's job to help athletes recognize their progress and successes. Was Jim Cherpes successful? Absolutely. He also had the coach's admiration for not giving up. You can bet that Jim Cherpes hasn't forgotten that day, either.

A recent picture with Don Barnbrook

The following year Riley won the City Indoor, beating Central 58 to 46, and Adams beat Central in the Outdoor meet, with Riley third and Washington fourth. Maybe we should have made A.B. stay another year.

Don Barnbrook followed A.B. Meyer. "Barney" was a senior at John Adams when I was a junior at Central. He played basketball, qualified for the state meet in the high hurdles and high jump, and had a good background and knowledge of track. Barney and I taught Biology across the hall from each other. He was particularly adept at talking to athletes with problems, and he had good insights, which made him a valuable resource. He was also the freshman basketball coach, and eventually transferred to Adams to become basketball coach there. He switched from biology to math in the classroom, which made me sad because he was such a good biology teacher. After Barney gave up track, I was hard pressed to find his replacement.

Bob Osborn

One of my friends on the faculty was a social studies teacher, Bob Osborn. Bob had no background in track, and to listen to him, didn't know much. Yet he cared enough to come out and help officiate our meets. Knowing how conscientious he was, the thought occurred to me that Ozzie might like to be assistant coach. When I approached him about it, his answer was predictable: "No! I don't know anything."

My reply to him was, "Don't worry about it. I will teach you all you need to know."

Bob finally agreed, and I was pleased. He started by timing workouts, and it wasn't long before he noticed other things that needed addressing. It wasn't long before he was accepted – and respected – as a coach.

Bob and I were together with the program until I left Riley track after the 1958 season. He left with me, and soon after moved to California to teach. I considered him very competent and productive as a coach, and I think getting him to accept the call was one of the best moves I made as head coach. I was very fortunate to have had three assistants as good as A.B. Meyer, Don Barnbrook, and Bob Osborn.

Most high school coaches have an assistant. Preferably it is someone with a track background. Too often, the assistant is not very knowledgeable in track - a teacher who volunteered or was talked into it, like Bob Osborn, (who turned out better than anyone could hope). Fortunately, track practices can be structured to make the best use of the inexperienced assistant. I had my own method to give on-the-job training while ensuring the best possible experience for the team.

A track practice has to be very organized, because the coaches are directing a large number of athletes (many very inexperienced) doing diverse activities taking place at the same time over a period of approximately an hour and a half. Workouts vary according to the time of season.

On Monday, I would post the workout schedule for the week. The assistant and student manager also got a copy. Each group (distances, middle distances, sprinters and hurdlers) would have work outs with repeated parts. For example, the distance men might have repeat 400's with a ten minute rest. I would time the first round of repeats, and then turn the timing over to the assistant. While I was timing, the assistant got the field event participants where they belonged and went over the day's work. After I finished the first round of timing, the assistant took over and I made the rounds of the field events, coaching at each stop. Usually, I started with the shot, then the pole vault, and finally the jumps. I tried to develop group leaders, usually upperclassmen, who then oversaw what had been worked on and then was being practiced. I then returned to the track to finish the timing and coach the sprinters and hurdlers, and check on the day's progress. The assistant would spend the rest of practice with the field events.

It wasn't long before the inexperienced assistant had learned enough to be a valuable member of the program.

9

Track: The Basic and Best Sport

You can't be a better runner unless you are willing to run and be beat. You've got to look for tough competition. You've got to want to beat the best.

Grete Waitz, distance runner

Track and Field is the oldest sport. The activities found in today's track and field go back to early times. Running, throwing, and jumping are activities that at one time were involved in basic survival and created competitive situations. Since the basic movements – running, throwing, jumping – can be done by almost anyone with some degree of success, it stands to reason that there is a place for *everyone* somewhere in track and field. All it takes is the proper effort and attitude for people to find their niche. Obviously, different participants will achieve different levels of success, but anyone can work, improve, and achieve personal bests. They don't have to star on the varsity track team, but they can be out there doing their best, gaining the advantages that track affords, whether on the varsity, junior varsity, or "B" team. In track, no one is ever cut for lack of ability. I coached eight years at Riley High School and spent 16 years as an assistant coach at Notre Dame, and I cannot remember an instance when someone was cut for lack of ability. The only time people were cut was for lack of attendance. In other words, athletes cut themselves by not being there.

One year at Riley, we had 92 boys turn out for the team, and they all participated in our first meet. That marked the birth of the "B" team in track, since the opposing team had the same situation we did. Whoever didn't run varsity ran "B" team. Everyone did something. Over the course of the season, we had a few drop out, but the majority stayed. All were encouraged to work toward improving their personal bests, regardless of how good they were. I remember vividly during one of our high school meets, the whole team lined the track, cheering on the worst miler we had as he struggled to finish.

Track is a social sport. In football and basketball, opposing teams have separate locker rooms. They run out on the field and warm up at opposite ends. They play the game, leave the field, and go home. The team benches are usually across the field from each other. There is no chance for interaction among the athletes. In track, teams usually will share a locker room, especially at large meets. Athletes mingle in the locker room, on the track as they warm up, and between events. They get to know each other by name, and over the course of an athlete's career, they become acquainted with most of their competition and find they are pretty fine people.

Everything I just said about track is especially true in cross country. One year our Conference meet was at Valparaiso, about 70 miles away. All four South Bend schools shared the same bus. The Adams coach, Ralph Powell, brought along a bushel of apples for everyone to share on the way home. The year Riley won the conference meet, we were elated going home, and friends from the other schools shared our joy. Their attitude was, "as long as we couldn't win, we're glad you did." This was possible because we all knew and liked each other. Once the race was over – and the competition between the schools was fierce – we were friends again. This kind of situation is possible very easily in track and cross country.

One thing that should be mentioned is that track and field affords a participant the chance to form memories that will last a lifetime. However, in order to form these memories, the person has to participate. Athletes don't realize that this is the chance of a lifetime. They are in high school only once. This opportunity will never come their way again. Too often high school students think they have to get a job in order to either buy a car or support a car. What kind of memories will these experiences provide fifty years down the road? Wouldn't activities provided by the school be much better? Would you rather remember anchoring a winning relay team against the school's big rival or the size of a paycheck that quickly disappeared at the nearest gas station? Of course, track is not the only source of these memories. Other sports, band, orchestra, various school clubs, and, yes, even the school play, all provide these opportunities. Students should take advantage of them.

Assessing our Record

There are many ways to gauge success. If athletes grow in strength, health, and confidence through the program, then it has been a success. If athletes improve their speed and form, reach personal bests, and learn to pull out every bit of potential to gain their goals, then the program is a success. If people develop friendships and memories that last the years, then the program is a success. However, there are more objective ways to gauge competitive success, and that is to see how the team compares to those they compete against.

Looking at the eight years that I was track coach, it was easy to see where we came up short and where we did well. Riley had some successes, notably winning the City Indoor and the City Outdoor meets in 1952, and the City Indoor in 1953. We were able to beat Central in a dual meet in 1952. Riley didn't have a history of beating Central, so that was a big achievement.

The easiest way to look at things objectively is to check the statistics.

The Statistics

Over all, during my eight years the Wildcats won 34 dual meets and lost 27. Against the other South Bend schools, we won 3 of 9 against Central, 5 of 6 against Adams, 7 of 10 against Washington, and 2 of 2 against St. Joseph's, a new Catholic school. That gave us a record of 17 wins and 10 losses against the other South Bend Schools. Now weigh that against 0 and 5 against neighboring Mishawaka, 0 and 3 against Elkhart, and 0 and 3 against LaPorte.

We did well against other schools that we had run over the years. They included Michigan City, Washington Clay, Lakeville, New Carlisle, Culver Military Academy, and Plymouth. We were 2-4 against Michigan City, 4-2 against CMA, and 3-0 against Plymouth. The meets with Lakeville and New Carlisle were very early season warm-up meets. These two schools were small county schools that didn't have much of a chance against the larger Riley, but they had several individuals who benefited from better competition.

In 1954, New Carlisle scored seven first places against us. Their big star in that meet was Don Coddens, who won the 100, 220, 440, and the long jump. Don went on to coach boys' and girls' basketball at Riley. Our schedule also included nine triangular meets. We finished first in four, second in two, and third in two. Schools involved in the triangular meets that we hadn't met in duals were Hobart, Warsaw, Nappanee, and Bremen.

Note: See Appendix E for top performances.

One of the problems we encountered was a general lack of speed, not only on the track team, but also in other sports. During this period, the football team suffered hard times as well, because team speed is important in that sport also.

The gym teachers cooperated and screened the gym classes for the hidden ones who were fleet of foot, yet undiscovered. There just weren't any. In track, that made us weak in the sprints and the 440, and once we got beyond John Abell, the low hurdles. Riley went into meets with the distance runners and field events as our strength to carry the day. Weakness in the speed events is hard to overcome in a dual meet. Fortunately, our successful cross country program provided a steady supply of fine distance runners.

Riley did have a few good sprinters. Gary Monus and Ron Walling did a fine job in the sprints during the time they were on the team. Walling even went to the State Meet, although he didn't place. Just getting there was an accomplishment. It is ironic that in eight years the ex-sprinter coach was only able to produce one or two sprinters that were a threat. If the speed is there, it's there. If it isn't, there isn't much you can do about it.

One indication of a general lack of team speed was the fact that we weren't able to put together good relay teams for the bigger meets, especially in the mile relay. We did have one decent half mile relay, but one in eight years isn't enough. In 1954, the half mile relay of Jack Kudlaty, Joe Meszaras, Chuck Kalwitz, and John Abell finished second in the East-West Conference meet in Elkhart, with an unofficial time of 1:33.7. Later in the season they finished first in an Inter-conference Meet in Kokomo, Indiana, winning with a time of 1:33.9, a Riley school record. The meet was between the Northern Indiana Conference and the North Central Conference. Lack of team speed hurt Riley dearly. Let's face it – speed is the key to the running events.

Strategies

A coach spends much time assigning the team members to the proper events for the meets. It is coach-against-coach, as one tries to outwit the other. Over time, each coach knows the opposition almost as well as his own team. By far, the fastest and best runner we had was our hurdler, John Abell. John could be expected to win the high and low hurdles. Conventional wisdom would have him, as our fastest runner, anchor the half mile relay. The problem was, we didn't have three others good enough to win with John. So instead of wasting John in the relay, I would use him in the 220, which he would usually win. In a dual meet, John Abell would give us 15 points (three firsts) instead of 10 (two firsts in the hurdles). This tactic is an example of switching runners to overcome a lack of team speed.

One year we had a tough meet coming up with the John Adams Eagles on their track. It promised to be a close meet, and by my reckoning it could have gone either way. I had gone over the meet, event by event, and we would have to come through in places we weren't used to in order to win. All of a sudden, the weekend before the meet, I had a great idea. We would have a contest on the team, where each team member would predict the final score of the meet. The one who came the closest would get a prize of some sort. Now, no one was going to predict that we would lose. That meant that each man was going to have to find where enough points would come from for us to win.

Each athlete then went over the meet, event by event, seeing where he had to score for a Wildcat win. Each team member figured out what it would take to win and, by golly, he wasn't going to cost us the meet by not scoring what he needed. When the meet came, I don't think the Eagles knew what hit them. Riley blew them away – almost doubled the score on them. I think that gimmick would work only once a year or so, but it was fun and, hopefully, each athlete would start to do it on his own for every meet, just like the coach.

Achievers

Although we didn't have powerhouse teams, we had some outstanding individual performers over the years. We had nine athletes advance to the State Finals in Indianapolis and six of them placed. Two stood out as the best of the best.

Dick Liechty, a 1953 graduate, pole vaulted, long jumped, and even high jumped when needed. His main event was the pole vault. His winning vault won the City Outdoor meet for Riley over Central. Dick had a fine grasp of the fundamentals of vaulting and was willing to share his knowledge with his teammates.

At the time, the poles in use were Swedish steel, which had replaced aluminum and bamboo. Soon fiberglass poles replaced the steel pole, and that completely revolutionized the event. With the steel pole, there wasn't much "whip," and the vaulter had to do a handstand at the top of his vault to enable him to clear the bar and let him drop into the pit. With the fiberglass pole, after planting the pole in the box, the vaulter leaned back on the pole, putting a good bend in it, which then whipped the vaulter up and over. The vaulter would need to stay close to the pole on the way up and pull up and turn and drop over the bar. It is my opinion, and it's one that many share, that there should be two sets of records for the pole vault: one using the fiberglass pole, and the other for everything else. I am certain that if Dick Liechty had used a fiberglass pole, he would have gone higher than 12'3". In 1952 he was in a 9-way tie for fifth in the State Meet at 11' 1", but in 1953, he finished second with 12'.

John Abell, way in front of the pack as usual.

John Abell was the best high school hurdler I had ever seen. He had natural form, something that he had to have been born with, and he was a very smooth runner with sprinter speed. John wasn't quick; he was just fast - and there is a difference. The hurdles are nothing more than a sprint with hurdles spaced along the way. You could have perfect hurdle form, and if you weren't fast, you wouldn't score. In reality, it is impossible to have perfect hurdle form if you can't run fast. It takes speed to get proper position over the hurdle in order to drive the lead leg down over the hurdle and get the proper body lean to maintain speed between hurdles. John did all this naturally, and the only place where John needed some work was driving out of the blocks at the start. This is where his coach helped.

John was state champion in the low hurdles in 1953 with the time of :20.2, and state champion in both the high and low hurdles in 1954, winning the highs in :14.8 and the lows in :19.5. John Abell has been inducted into both the Riley High School Athletic

Hall of Fame and the Indiana Track Hall of Fame. Both groups knew what they were doing.

In the 1970s, Dick Fosbury introduced a new form in the high jump called, not surprisingly, the "Fosbury Flop." Using this form, the jumper cleared the bar on his back. The high jump hasn't been the same since. Prior to the '70s, jumpers used either the straddle jump, where the jumper went over on his stomach, or the western roll, where the jumper cleared the bar on his side.

Riley had two high jumpers go to State: Dick Whitaker in 1954 and Chuck Kalwitz in 1955. Dick also was a good high hurdler, and Chuck a long jumper and relay man. At State, Whitaker had a 2-way tie for third at 6' 1", and Kalwitz a 3-way tie for fifth at 5'11". Both Whitaker and Kalwitz used the straddle. How high could they have gone using the "flop"?

In 1952, Jerry Jacobs went to State in the shot put, placing third with a put of 50' 5½". Jerry was a very hard worker. The basic form in the shot had undergone change also. Using the old form, the athlete would get into the ring facing the side; with the new form, he would start facing the back. The new form produced better distance than the old. Jerry was another natural athlete who also played football, and he adapted to the new form very well. I am sorry that Jerry was on the team only two years when I was coach.

Riley also had two athletes go to State in the 880: Ralph Long in 1952 and Jim Mahoney in 1953. Ralph finished fifth with a time of 2:01.8, his personal best. Ralph's problem was a lack of basic speed. His last race was also his fastest, and he felt good about that. Mahoney didn't place at all. His problem was that he was a late bloomer and needed additional strength and maturity. He had the same problem his coach had in high school.

We had two other athletes go to State: Louie Cass in the mile and Ron Walling in sprints. Louie was a distance runner who was a leader on the best cross country team the school ever had up to that point. Ron Walling was a hard working sprinter with a best time of :10.2 in the 100, and :22.7 in the 220 (a Riley School record). Both of those times were faster than what his coach did in high school. We didn't have much backup to go along with Ron, which was unfortunate. There were also some "super sprinters" in the area who could run under 10 seconds for the 100, which tended to overshadow a good sprinter like Ron. However, the joy of track is not in the winning or losing. It is in the process of growth and meeting one's best potential.

10
Cross Country Coaching

Just hurry back, son... hurry back.
Frank "Hurry Back" Hill, Northwestern Track Coach

Cross country is a companion sport to track. It is a distance event that is run off the track. Back when I was coaching at Riley, the distance was two miles, and our main course was the Erskine Golf Course in South Bend, located a little over a mile from the school. Occasionally, we would run on the Studebaker Golf Course, which was next to the school. Erskine was far superior, since it was hilly and was a larger course. Other courses used for cross country were city parks, large parking lots, fields, and back roads, but by far, the golf course was the most common course.

The distance for a cross country meet in Indiana today is 5K, or 3.1 miles. A cross country team officially consists of seven runners, with the first five finishers producing the score for the team. The sixth and seventh runners are referred to as "pushers," for if they finish ahead of any of the first five of the other team, it will increase the score of the other team, which can affect the results of the meet.

The low score wins in cross country. Each finisher receives the score for the place he finishes – first receives one, second place gets two, third three, and so on. If a team has its first five finishers

93

finish ahead of the first runner of the opposition, the team's score would be 15 (1,2,3,4,5 – these numbers totaled equal 15). If the two pushers also beat the first five of the other team, the winning team would still have 15, but the opposition's score would now be 50 (8, 9, 10, 11, 12) instead of 40 (6, 7, 8, 9, 10). Most meets do not finish this one-sided. Most teams have several runners who can hold their own and the finish is a nice mix of runners, with meet scores of 27-28 common.

The scoring system works the same for larger meets. The State Sectional had between 10 and 15 teams, and large conference meets like the Northern Indiana would have twenty. In 1956, Riley won the Northern Indiana Conference meet with 71 points, which was actually a rather high score for that meet. The last place team had a score of 565. That means that their first 5 finishers finished an average of over 100. I would say that team needed work.

There is an interesting fact that applies to dual meets. If a team finishes 1, 2, 3 in a dual meet, there is no way the team can lose the meet. The other team could pack in the next 7 together, and they would still lose the meet. The score would be 29 (1, 2, 3, 11, 12) to 30 (4, 5, 6, 7, 8). Cross country is clearly a team sport, and in big meets especially, a team is no better than its 5th man. You will see shortly how that works.

When a totally inexperienced runner first came out for the team, there was a procedure that I used to keep him from getting discouraged and to bring him along slowly. The first workouts for the beginner would be to go out and run until he was "pleasantly tired" – tired but not exhausted, tired but not in pain. By alternating running with walking during these workouts, before long he would be running at a faster sustainable pace. When the beginner started working with the main group, he needed to follow one of our main rules: no one runs alone. Always run with someone, with one pushing the other along. The idea was that eventually a group would form that would run together, pushing each other along. This would form a pack, which is the type of team that wins meets.

I consider Riley's 1956 team to be Riley's finest up to that date. The first four runners were pretty well set: Dave Fritz, Louie Cass, Rodger McKee, and Jim Manuszak. We needed a strong fifth man. We had two good candidates: Bill Barnes and Ken Selby. Barnes and Selby were instructed to stay with the pack no matter what, and the pack was instructed not to let Barnes and Selby fall back. Slow down if you must, but keep Bill and Ken with you. In time, this strategy paid off. We had a strong top five to compete anywhere. It was strange, though, that Barnes and Selby never ran a good race in the same meet. Either Bill or Ken would have a good day. Fortunately, they never had a bad day at the same time.

The best of the best team. Back row, Bill Barnes, Bob Smith, Ken Selby, Charles Kachel. Front row: Louie Cass, Dave Fritz, Rodger McKee, Jim Manuszak. Larry Severin is not pictured. *Courtesy of the South Bend School Corporation*

**The law runneth forward and back –
And the strength of the pack is the wolf
And the strength of the wolf is the pack.**
Rudyard Kipling, English Poet/Novelist

Along with training to form a pack, our team also learned to set their pace so they would always know where they were timewise. In every meet they ran, they had a goal for a certain time, and then by knowing their own pace, they would know where they were at the various markers: the half mile, one mile, etc. This prevented them from being pulled out at the start of a race by the "rabbits," eager runners that sprint out in front and then fade fast. Inexperienced runners drawn out by that tactic don't run their own race. They are running someone else's race by not knowing their own pace. Our teams at Riley were very good teams that worked hard to form a strong pack, so they had success.

Coaching Methods

Over the years, I got to know many coaches. Each had a different coaching style that had varying strengths and weaknesses. There is no single best technique to coach. One thing that all good coaches possess is the belief in hard work. Hard work produces conditioning, and conditioning produces wins. Wins produce confidence, and confidence makes it easier to work harder, which makes it easier to win. The ultimate goal is to get a team that expects to win because they know they are "better" than their opponents. This is confidence backed by hard work. This was especially true in cross country.

There are as many coaching methods as there are coaches. A coach may be a hard nosed slave driver and achieve success if his team responds to his methods. Another coach using the same tactics might drive some of his boys off the team. A coach must adjust his workouts to the abilities of his runners. A team of young underclassmen would be handled differently than a team of seasoned seniors. I can't help but remember my own experience when Coach Anson had to pick me up off the track! As a coach, I did like to push my team hard, because a young runner cannot know how fast he can run until he is pushed to it. Along with the pushing, the coach has to know the limitations (physical strength, natural stamina, etc.) of the individual runners.

There are many ways to make a good runner better. One would be to teach the runner his pace. A good runner always knows where he is with regard to time during a race. During practice, having paced work lets the runners know how long it takes them to run a certain distance at a certain speed. Make it easy to start, having checkpoints at ¼ lap, ½ lap, and one lap. Once they know their pace, it is easy to regulate the expected speed over the workout distance. By increasing the expected speed, the coach can push them to greater speeds.

In cross country, we would discuss what the speed goal was for the coming meet. The goal should be a little faster each meet, and knowing the pace makes this easier to do. I would expect them to run the first ¾ of the race at their expected speed, and the last ¼ by the competition. If they run properly, their times should improve each meet.

Leveraging Competition

Another way to improve is to run tough competition. Know who you are running, and "go get'em." Again, know your pace and stay with it. That can be tough. You don't want your opponent to get away from you, but you don't want to deviate from your race pace too early in the race.

One of our biggest rivals in cross country was Mishawaka High School. We would run them in a conference dual during the season, as well as in the East West Conference meet and the State

Sectional. I also liked to run them in our opening meet, since I knew they would be tough, and we wanted to know what they had so we would know where improvements had to be made. I'm sure the Mishawaka coach, Ralph Burgess, had the same thing in mind.

Riley's 1956 cross country team was a good one, but that year we lost to Mishawaka in our opening meet 26-30. Mishawaka had a great athlete, LeRoy Johnson. He was a great high jumper and basketball player as well as runner. We soon learned that "as LeRoy Johnson goes, so goes Mishawaka." LeRoy was the winner in that opening meet, with a time of 10:33. Riley's Cass and Fritz were second and third with times of 10:36 and 10:38. When our conference dual came around two weeks later, it was a double dual with Riley, Mishawaka, and Michigan City at Michigan City. We decided our strategy would be to keep the pressure on Johnson right from the start. Our third and fourth men, Rodger McKee and Jim Manuszak, both had the confidence to run with LeRoy. They did a super job and stayed right with him. With those two with him, Johnson couldn't worry about Cass and Fritz, who went on to place second and third in the meet. The individual winner of the race was Hutmacher of Michigan City. Johnson finished 7th, with a time of 10:25; McKee was 8th with 10:26, with Manuszak 9th with 10:27. The three of them finished within two seconds of each other, and Riley won the meet 26-29 against Mishawaka, and 24-31 against Michigan City. Riley went on to finish the season with a dual record of 11-1. That opening loss to Mishawaka was the Wildcat's only loss.

Later Riley won the East-West Conference meet at Valparaiso with 71 points. Mishawaka was second with 84. In the State Sectional, Riley won with 79, the Mishawaka team was fourth with 109. Riley then went on to place sixth in the state meet in Indianapolis.

I am convinced that the early loss to Mishawaka set up our season. This was an example of a veteran team ready and willing to be pushed, because they knew what the rewards would be. Given their ability, they achieved at the highest level possible. Their coach was proud of them.

Riley won the Conference in 1954 and 1956, the Sectional in 1955 and 1956, and the City Meet from 1951 through 1956. Our dual meet record from 1951 through 1957 was 62 won, 25 lost, with one tie. Since we had so many runners so close in ability, I will list them in Appendix F, the top seven (on average) from top to bottom for each year.

Photo taken Oct 18, 1956. The whole team.
Back row: Coach Bob Smith, Larry Severin, John Odusch, Lyle Robinson, Don Hanish, George Page, Herman West, Charles Kachel
Front Row: Bill Barnes, Dave Fritz, Louie Cass, Rodger McKee, Jim Manuszak, Ken Selby *Photo courtesy of the South Bend School Corporation*

The members of the teams all had a good sense of humor, and we enjoyed each other, which added to the fun. Dave Fritz was among the smallest and fastest runners we had. I doubt if Dave weighed 100 pounds. In the Conference meet at Valparaiso, there were 20 teams, with a total of 140 runners. Louie Cass finished third, with Fritz tenth. Dave made the crack that he ran the first half mile before he got his feet on the ground! A stretch, maybe, but not by much. This meet was in 1956, and our other finishers were Jim Manuszak 16th, Rodger McKee 19th, and Ken Selby 23rd. Our pushers also placed high. Bill Barnes was 38th, and Larry Severin was 68th. Considering there were 140 running, you can see that our "pack running" paid off, and our team did well, winning with 71 points. We also won the Conference in 1954 using the same tactic. Bill Manuszak was 9th, Roger Overmyer 14th, Jim Smith 16th, Ken Jackson 17th, and Ken Ford 26th for 82 points. Our pushers were Louie Cass 43rd and Bill Thrasher 45th. With 140 runners, all seven did their job.

Transitions

Graduation took the top five from the previous year's team, so 1957 was a rebuilding year. The Wildcats of '57 were coming along when a flu epidemic struck the school and all but leveled the cross country team. We didn't have enough healthy runners to have a practice, since this was a rather severe strain of the flu. We had the City Meet, the Conference Meet, and the Sectional coming up, and our boys were still sick or in a weakened condition - in no shape to tackle the work necessary to run those meets. After discussing the situation with our principal, John Byers, we decided that Riley would withdraw from our remaining meets and call it a season. We thought stress put on our flu-weakened team would be detrimental to the boys' health, so the season ended with a dual record of 8 and 7.

1958 marked my eighth year as track coach and was my eighth year in the classroom as well. My assignment had been mainly seventh grade science, and I learned a lot. There is nothing like teaching a subject to help you learn. The first two years I also had a Health class with the seventh graders. The seventh graders had an extra period with no class to schedule for them. Mr. Dake, the principal at the time, thought it would be a good idea for them to have a Health class, and he also thought it would be a good idea for me to teach it. There was no course outline, no book. I was on my own. It was quite an experience and it lasted a year.

After teaching the seventh graders for five years, I had the opportunity to move into Biology. I was ready for that. I then spent the remainder of my 39-year career teaching Biology, which was a good move for me. Then in 1958, Mr. Forrest Marsh, the second-year biology teacher, retired. That wonderful veteran teacher probably knew more than all of us young'uns combined. He also knew a lot about fishing, and we had spent a lot of time between classes talking about fishing. He did most of the talking, and I did most of the listening. He imparted knowledge, not only about fishing, but biology and nature as well.

Teaching second-year biology intrigued me, so I applied for the position. Evidently, the administration was satisfied with my work in first-year biology, because they gave me the second-year class. Teaching that class took much more preparation at a higher level, so I thought I could do a better job if I gave up track. Not only would I need the extra time, but I was getting a little stressed from coaching. Coaching in high school takes its toll, so after much thought and discussion, I decided to give up coaching track and cross country at Riley.

When that decision was made, I thought my coaching days were over. That was it. I boxed up my coaching and track technique books and shipped them to my brother in California, who was just getting started in teaching and track coaching. Paul Frazier, another Riley biology teacher, took over the track and cross country team from me.

A sad note: a week after he retired, Forrest Marsh went into the hospital and died a short time later. He had a brain tumor and was unable to enjoy any of his retirement. His passing was hard on all of us. Every year he would talk about retirement but never did. There is a lesson here.

Success

After making the decision to leave high school coaching, it was fitting to look back over those years and make a self-appraisal of my success or failure as a coach. What criteria should be used? Should it be the won-lost record? Should it be the number of athletes participating? Should it be the number of athletes scoring in the meets? It is easy to come up with all kinds of figures to support any criterion, but in any evaluation there are always intangibles that make it almost impossible to evaluate any program. A case can be made for the number of participants being the most important factor. After all, if the program didn't have something valuable to offer, the students wouldn't turn out.

Over the eight year period, an average of 39 athletes per year scored at least one point over the course of the season, counting both varsity and "B" teams. The numbers ranged from 24 in 1951, to a high of 49 in 1954. I don't have any figures for those who spent the season and didn't score at least one point, but there weren't many.

In cross country, we had an average of 18 out for the team over seven years, with all of them winning something. As was pointed out earlier, no one was ever cut for lack of ability.

Each person on the team would have an opinion on whether the team was a success or not. The feelings and opinions of the slowest sprinter would be as good as mine, because all of our athletes had different experiences. They all have their own memories that they carry with them. If I, as their coach, gave them the opportunity to form good memories, then I was successful. If not, then I was not so successful.

Occasionally I will run into one of my former athletes, many of whom are retired or close to it. When I do, I never remember how many points he scored, or how many races he won, or even what year he graduated, but what I DO remember is what kind of person he was. I can honestly say that, thinking back, I have only positive thoughts of those who ran on my teams.

One of the highlights of my career came last summer, when I was invited to the 50th wedding anniversary open house of Chuck McGeath, one of my early distance men. Also present was Chuck's best man, Dick Liechty. It gave the old coach a real lift after all these years, and the open house added to my great track memories.

11
A Surprise Return

Get Back! Get Back! Get Back to where you once belonged.
The Beatles

Shortly after my graduation at Notre Dame, Doc Handy resigned as track coach. He had come from Iowa, and he returned there, but no one knew exactly why he left Notre Dame. His last team was hard hit by graduation, having lost John Helwig, Bill Fleming, Jim Miller, and me. We held ten all-time Notre Dame records.

Within a short time, Alex Wilson, the coach at Loyola of Chicago, replaced Doc. Alex was a Notre Dame graduate and Olympic runner from Canada, who had competed in the 1928 and 1932 Olympics. He had held the Notre Dame record in the quarter mile for many years. He was also an excellent coach, doing a lot with a few talented runners. During my last two years at Notre Dame, Loyola had a mile relay team that beat Notre Dame with regularity. It was during this time that I got to know Alex.

During my time coaching at Riley, I had helped Alex as an official at the Notre Dame meets, usually serving as a finish judge. The only events that were hard to call were the hurdles and sprints, which shouldn't have surprised me. I knew firsthand how close those races could be. Being a volunteer official enabled me to meet and get to know the other officials. They were mostly professors, and they all helped because of their love of the sport. No one got paid. Alex always said that they would be insulted if they were offered pay. The only paid official was the starter.

Every year before the start of the season, Alex would invite all the officials to a dinner at Franky's Restaurant in Niles, Michigan. He couldn't have picked a better place, because Franky's was well known for their ham sandwiches. That was all the pay we received, but Notre Dame's track officials were well respected by everyone coming in to meet the Irish.

After I had resigned as coach at Riley, I never expected to coach again, and was absorbed in my class schedule consisting of first and second year biology classes. My coaching was behind me; my earlier dream was fulfilled. Then one evening I received a phone call from Alex Wilson, asking me if I would be interested in being the freshman cross country coach at Notre Dame. In fact, he did more than ask if I'd be interested – he asked me if I would do it. This offer was surprising and unexpected, and I told him it would have to be cleared by the South Bend School Corporation. The coaching would be done after my high school responsibilities were over each day.

I thought about it for a couple of days and decided that I would try it, so I cleared it with the school authorities. Alex was pleased that I would be working with him, and thus began an experience and relationship with Alex that lasted 14 years at Notre Dame and then continued on for the rest of his life.

I was considered part-time by Notre Dame, which meant no perks or benefits, although I was Alex's only assistant and was there six or seven days per week. Being an assistant at Notre Dame was less demanding on my time than high school coaching, although it was every day. All I did was coach. I had nothing to do with equipment or aches and pains (that was the trainer's job), but I did get involved in knowing the athletes better.

The group I worked with consisted of seven freshmen, and I enjoyed being with them. The team practiced on the Burke Golf Course on campus at Notre Dame and ran apart from the varsity cross country team. For the first time, I became acquainted with a postal meet. During the fall we had two postal meets. The first was with Drake. On a specific day, our team ran two miles for time and the times were recorded. On the same day in Des Moines, Drake's freshmen did the same. The times were exchanged (usually by phone, although at first they were mailed, hence the term postal meet), and the scores were determined using the exchanged times.

Notre Dame's times were 9:49.6, 10:06.4, 10:17, 10:18, 10:27.3, 10:53.9, and 11:34. Drake's times were 9:22, 10:13, 10:17, 10:33.5, 10:53, 11:05, and 11:19.5. Assigning places to these times, Notre Dame was second, third, tie for fifth, seventh and eighth for 25½ points. Drake was first, fourth, a tie for fifth, ninth, tenth, twelfth and thirteenth for 29½ points. Notre Dame was the winner of the meet. Later in the fall, Notre Dame defeated Colgate in a postal meet 19-38.

The freshmen had a triangular meet at Notre Dame with Western Michigan and Bowling Green. The Broncos with 21 points defeated the Irish with 41 and Bowling Green with 72. Notre Dame's season ended with a Central Collegiate Conference meet in Chicago, a three-mile race with no team title. With the ending of the freshman season, it was time to move into the field house and join the upper classmen for the indoor season. That also marked the end of my work with the freshmen.

As it turned out, my tenure with the freshmen cross country team was a trial for me. Alex wanted to see how I panned out with the freshmen cross country runners before he made his next move, which was to offer me the position of assistant track coach, starting right away. Alex must have been satisfied with the progress we made, although with the quality individuals on the frosh team, that was going to happen anyway. I did work hard and never missed a day's practice. Alex and I also hit it off personally. Of course, anyone who couldn't get along with Alex Wilson had something wrong with them.

I coached for Alex until he retired in 1972, and we remained friends until he died in 1994. He was a very positive force in my life, and I tried to emulate him whenever I could. Though I was part time as far as Notre Dame was concerned, I was full time as far as Alex was concerned. My duties covered a multitude of responsibilities. I was in charge of the freshmen paperwork (gym excuses, etc.), keeping a daily record of their attendance. I was still freshman coach, since we still had freshman meets. I helped Alex with practice, paying special attention to the sprinters and hurdlers. It was wonderful the way Alex and I worked together. I was a detail person, and Alex was great with the big picture. I was good at remembering names. Al wasn't once he got beyond the point getters. Everybody had a coach who knew his name, which was important to the freshmen.

After Alex and I had been together a while, he added to my duties something that turned out to be my biggest job. He appointed me "official worrier" when it came to the meets. I was a natural. Alex never worried about a thing, at least outwardly. When he did worry, it was always over something that really counted, not everyday trivialities. Working for Alex Wilson was like getting a lesson in life every day.

I remember one day we discussed a trackman who was giving us trouble. There was a lack of cooperation and acceptance of responsibility.

"Just remember," Alex said, "We didn't make him like this, and we have to deal with him the way he is. If he doesn't want to cooperate, then he can move on."

Early in his career, Alex taught high school and eventually couldn't stand it. I asked him one day the difference between coaching high school and college. He answered that you can sit down and reason with a college student, whereas you couldn't with a high school student. Alex was referring to discussions on workouts and other issues relating to track. The high schooler didn't have enough experience to discuss much. The college runner did have the experience.

I can remember Alex discussing workouts with one of his upper classmen, and the two of them came up with an adjusted schedule that turned out to be advantageous to the runner and ultimately the team.

When I was a student/athlete at Notre Dame, freshmen were eligible for the varsity. The years immediately following World War II were unique, because most of the students were older and more mature due to their experiences in the service. Their main objective was to get through school as quickly as possible and get on with their lives. While in school, they wanted to experience as many activities as possible. Unlike most of the veterans, I was only nineteen when entering Notre Dame, and I didn't feel that being on the varsity track team was an undue burden.

By the time I returned to Notre Dame in the fall of 1958, freshman eligibility had been revoked, and freshmen couldn't be on the varsity team. In the early 1970s, freshman eligibility was restored, so during my tenure I was able to observe firsthand the differences between freshman eligibility and ineligibility.

I believe very strongly that if colleges were truly concerned about the academic welfare of the athletes, freshmen would not be eligible for varsity. Their first year would be spent acclimating to campus life as students. They would be able to spend their freshman year on the freshman track team, using the year as one of development and exploration in a program geared especially for them. A college freshman is nothing more than a high school graduate three months old. With a separate freshman program, a day's practice could be missed to prepare for a tough exam without feeling that chances of making the team were compromised.

Whenever the legendary professor, Dr. Emil T. Hofman, had one of his famous chemistry exams coming up, track attendance was hard hit with the coach's blessing.

Another problem that occasionally surfaced was homesickness, which affected a few of our athletes. If there was a freshman coach available to address such problems, it would help the athletes' adjustment to college and to track. Although every case was different, I usually approached homesickness with the observation that some homesickness is expected. I put a positive spin on it by telling the young man that a little homesickness could be construed as a good thing, for that meant that he had a home worth missing, and we took it from there and worked through his problem. More often than not, the problem disappeared.

Another advantage of having a freshman coach was that it provided someone for the athlete just to talk to. I can remember all kinds of discussions, and even if the student disagreed with my observations, he at least knew why he thought what he did. It was fun and I enjoyed it, as I borrowed a page from Alex Wilson's book.

During freshman ineligibility, we had about 40 freshmen on the team. We had freshman meets for them, both postal and on-site. Western Michigan would usually bring their team down once a year, sometimes twice. Some years we had a triangular meet with Western Michigan and Grand Rapids Junior College. One year Ohio State came to Notre Dame for an outdoor meet. One year I took the team to Purdue for a freshman relay meet. That was the first time that Alex sent me off campus with a team, and it wouldn't be the last.

Having so many on the team, most of them walk-ons, gave us a chance to develop some depth on the varsity that we hadn't had for a long time. The walk-on had a full school year to develop into a productive athlete. Once freshman eligibility was restored, the number of walk-ons plummeted from around 40 down to ten or twelve. If a student's choice was to make the varsity his freshman year or do nothing, too many chose to do nothing. Most of our freshmen then were scholarship men, and most of them did make the varsity. Attempts to recruit enough walk-ons to bring us back to our previous numbers did not succeed. We were much better off when freshmen were not eligible, better off by any yardstick you want to use.

Traveling Coach

The vast majority of our meets were run on Saturday, and the only time I would travel with the team was if it was a one-day trip. Friday was a travel day, and it was a school day for me, which meant that any time Notre Dame traveled on Friday, I was left behind. There were a few exceptions to that, however.

One year Notre Dame was sending a small team to the Milwaukee Relays, and Alex had a meeting early in the afternoon with the meet committee. He took one of the relay teams with him. It was up to me to bring the other relay team to Milwaukee, and I wouldn't have to leave until after school. Right after school at Riley, I went out to Notre Dame and picked up the four boys. On the way out of town, we stopped at Bill Knapp's Restaurant for dinner then hit the road.

Now the four boys with me were all blessed with a sense of humor. Somewhere along the way, I picked up the reputation of being rather conservative, and my passengers took delight in back seat driving. Not only were they in the back seat, but also in the front. Little did they realize that something was going to happen that would provide them with enough joke fodder to last them, not only to Milwaukee, but the return trip.

After Chicago, the highway still had tollbooths, and I pulled up to one with my change all ready to make the unerring toss of the coins into the basket. You can probably guess what happened next.

I missed the basket entirely with all the coins. You can imagine the reaction of my passengers when that happened! Only the fact that they didn't want to spend the night at the tollbooth caused one of the lads to hop out of the car and quickly retrieve the coins, making a slam dunk into the basket, and we were on our way again. Needless to say, that little episode did not die quietly. We made it to Milwaukee on time and had a safe trip back to campus on Sunday. I like to think it was due to my conservatism.

One April Alex found that he was going to need surgery, which would keep him away from the team for three or four weeks. That would leave me in charge of the team, not only for practice, but also for two away meets. I had to take personal leave days from the high school in order to travel on Friday.

The first meet was the Kentucky Relays in Lexington, where we had a small team entered. It was not enough for a bus, but just right for the School's ten-passenger limo, and I would do the driving. This presented the team wags with a real dilemma. Here was a chance to harass the assistant coach (with a reputation for conservatism) or to play it straight to be sure we got there safe and sound. Those boys weren't college students for nothing, so we had a very uneventful trip. It wasn't hard to see the choice they made.

We stayed at the Ramada Inn, which was located on the other side of town from the track. The meet was an afternoon affair, so we had plenty of time to relax and get rested to run. Imagine my surprise when I was having breakfast with three of our runners at 8 a.m. when one of our distance men came in wearing his track sweat suit.

Runner: "Coach, can I go over to the track?"
Coach: "How are you going to get there?"
Runner: "I'm going to run over there."
Coach: "Do you mean that you will be running through heavy traffic in a strange town?"

Runner: "Yes, I guess so."

Coach: "I guess the answer is NO."

Runner: "Why not?"

Coach: "Because I am responsible for you and the answer is no."

Runner: "But…"

Coach: "What is there about 'NO' that you don't understand?"

That ended it, and I drove the runner to the meet with the team.

The next morning when I went to check out, the desk clerk told me the manager wanted to see me.

"Now what," I wondered.

The manager came out and told me that our group was the best-behaved group of college kids that had ever stayed there, and that I should be proud of them. I suggested he drop Moose Krause a note and relay that to him. I was proud of them.

The other away meet was in Oxford, Ohio, where we had a triangular meet with Miami University and Bowling Green. This time we took a full team and it was a bus trip. Unfortunately for us, Miami beat Notre Dame 74 to 65, with the Falcons close with 64. This was a meet where we went the day before and came home right after the meet. We stayed all night on the Miami campus in a big dormitory in the basement of one of the dorms. All of us, including me, slept in the same room. That was the first time I had slept in a dormitory since my navy days.

Again, the behavior of the team was exemplary, and again I was proud of them. I had always gotten along with the team, and finally realized that on both trips they had tried to make it as easy as possible for me. As I thought about that, it occurred to me that I couldn't think of one case of misbehavior away from campus on meet trips. It didn't matter who was coaching, whether it was Doc

Handy, Alex Wilson, or a two-meet sub, Bob Smith. The Notre Dame trackmen were classy individuals, a credit to the University.

During Alex's recovery, I would stop at his home following practice to keep him abreast of how things were going. I had no problem directing the workouts during his absence. After all, by this time I was an experienced coach. However, we were all glad when Alex was able to return to the team after his surgery and everything returned to normal.

One of the things that Alex wanted me to do was to bring a freshman home for dinner periodically. The purpose was to let the freshman know he was wanted and that we had an interest in him. I found this an interesting experience. One of the things I had experienced as a freshman was the attitude of others on the team toward South Bend. It might as well have been another planet, and I, being a native indigenous to the area, served as a lightning rod for all the gripes they had about South Bend: the weather, the climate, the local bus company, etc. It was as if they gave their hometown, wherever it was, a rating of 100% and South Bend was continually compared to that. Of course, it was next to impossible to compete.

Some students were interested in what a Hoosier was, and they were told to take a look. It was hard to separate what they really felt about northern Indiana and South Bend and what was just a poor attempt at humor. All most of them knew about South Bend was the bus route from the campus to downtown and they based everything on that. I must admit, there were times that their grousing wore a little thin.

One of the freshmen that I brought home was a sprinter named Bill Hurd. Bill was an extraordinary person, one of the most talented I have ever known. Not only was he fast, he set all the Notre Dame sprint records except the 220 yard straightaway (a race that was no longer run). He surpassed his coach's records easily, and I am glad that I was around to help coach him to do it. (Not that he needed any help.) Bill Hurd graduated in 1969, having won

113

monograms in 1967, 1968, and 1969. In both 1968 and 1969 he placed third in the NCAA 200 meter. In 1968 he placed fourth in the NCAA 100 meter, and in 1969, fifth in the 100 meter.

Bill Hurd, Bob Smith, and Ole Skarstein.
Photo courtesy of University of Notre Dame.

Not only was he a great athlete, but also a talented jazz musician on the saxophone. He graduated from the School of Engineering and then went to medical school, where he became an ophthalmologist. Using that skill, he has done humanitarian work in Africa. Bill is a credit to himself, his family, Notre Dame, and mankind.

Along with Bill Hurd, we had another outstanding sprinter, Ole Skarstein from Mo-i-Rana Norway. Mo-i-Rana is located just south of the arctic circle. Ole was on three recordsetting relay teams while at Notre Dame: the 440, the 880, and the sprint medley. Ole had a sense of humor, and we enjoyed one another. I got to know him well when he was in my sprinter group.

Ole was always trying to get me to speak Norwegian, and I even went so far as to get a book, *Say It In Norwegian*. After a brief period, my linguistic efforts came to naught. If I was to learn Norwegian, I would need more than Ole and the little book. "Hvordan sier De 'run fast'?" (How do you say 'run fast'?) That's all I needed to know.

I was the sprint and hurdle coach, since participants in these events needed individual attention, which Alex didn't have time to provide. I would work with my group of athletes, and whenever one of them got good enough, Alex would take them over. I didn't have Bill Hurd very long.

Over the years, Notre Dame has had many outstanding athletes who competed on the national and international level. One of these attended Notre Dame during my tenure as assistant. Rick Wohlhuter was one of the greatest runners ever to wear the gold and blue. To me, Rick was the epitome of what an athlete should be during his competitive years and later in life. While going through injury-induced disappointments, he was never discouraged and continued to practice with a positive attitude. It was during this injury period and recovery (for a foot and ankle injury) that I really got to know and appreciate Rick.

In 1969, Rick was on a two mile relay team that finished second in the NCAA indoor meet. The other runners were Mike McCann, Joe Quigley, and John Brady. In 1970 he finished first in the indoor NCAA 600 yds. Rick now had become a force in the sport. His most exciting race was finishing third in the 800 m. in the 1976 Montreal Olympics. It was close enough that on another day, he might have won.

A recent picture with Rick Wohlhuter.

Since Rick graduated in 1971, much of his success came after he left Notre Dame. In 1974, he won the prestigious Sullivan Award, which recognizes the country's top amateur athlete. In

1991, he was elected to the Track and Field Hall of Fame. Rick and his family live in Wheaton, IL, and over the years he has attended the Alumni reception following the Alex Wilson Invitational. Rick and his wife Kathy have two children, Charlie and Mary, and are successful parents, which is what you would expect.

An entire book could be written on the success stories of the trackmen who were on the team when I was Alex's assistant. They were not all stars, but were the good solid performers necessary for a good team. One such runner was Bob Hoover '64. Bob Hoover won three monograms and was a dependable quarter miler. Bob was one of my favorite discussion partners at practice. We enjoyed our conversations, and it's a shame we couldn't have solved the world's problems. Bob is now a nationally-known cancer researcher in Maryland.

Another successful runner was Keith Manville '66, with two monograms. He was a hurdler and a hard worker whose problem was a lack of sprinter speed. He and I "argued" for four years over his workouts, especially during fall track conditioning. He finally agreed to try the coach's way his senior year. We were both pleased when his senior year was his best. Keith is now a school administrator in Massachusetts.

Bob and Keith are only two examples; there were many others. My charges set several school records in the sprints and hurdles, including the shuttle hurdle, and the following relays: the 440 yard, 880 yard, sprint medley, and the mile relay. All of these recordsetting runners are listed in Appendix G. It should be noted that most of these records were set during the years when freshmen were ineligible for the varsity. The large number of freshmen contributed to the balance of the varsity and provided for the depth of the varsity (which contributed to the records).

Another good sprinter was Rich Vallicelli, who ran a :09.5 100 yard dash in 1971. His father followed Rich's career closely, so I got to know Arthur Vallicelli so well that he and Mrs. Vallicelli had dinner at our home. Arthur was a high school principal at Proviso West in Hillside, Illinois, outside of Chicago. I was very surprised when he offered me a job in their science department. Their facilities were better than Riley's, and the pay was higher. Before giving him an answer, we took a trip to check out the area, not only where I would teach, but also where we would live.

After we got home, we decided that we didn't want to live in such a congested area. Shortly after that, we bought five acres in the country near South Bend and constructed a home on it. We have never been sorry we decided to remain in South Bend. Strictly as a teacher, I probably would have been better off at Proviso West, but we had been looking for acreage for several years, and what we found near South Bend was exactly what we wanted. It was a biology teacher's dream, and we lived in the country for thirty years. Certainly I appreciated Arthur Vallicelli's faith in me as a teacher without ever seeing me teach. My association with Rich and his father were an enjoyment to me in my coaching career.

Another Decision Point

As time passed, Alex came closer to retirement, and it was time for me to step back and take a hard look at where I was going. Al was going to retire in 1972, and I would be 45 years old when he did. Moose Krause asked me if I would like to be considered for Alex's job.

I had taught at Riley High School for 22 years and I enjoyed my biology classes. I had been involved in track in some capacity for 28 years. Did I want to continue in track? I had met the goals that I had set for myself. Was it time to retire from track and devote all of my time to biology?

It was time for me to look at the pros and cons of coaching on the college level as a head coach. Coaching is teaching, but you have the responsibility for choosing your own class.

Recruiting is a major part of a head coach's job, and I didn't think I would enjoy that aspect of the position. First, you have to find the prospect. Next, you have to sell the school to the prospect, and then you have to sell the prospect to the school. Once the prospect is accepted by the school and enrolls, he has to attend classes and maintain his eligibility. My experience with recruiting was very limited. In all of my time with Alex, he had sent me on only one recruiting trip, calling on a sprinter from Highland, Indiana. After talking with the lad for a few minutes, it was evident to me that he and Notre Dame would not be a good fit. He ended up at Purdue and was never heard of again (in track, that is).

There is little room for error in recruiting because the number of scholarships is limited and a coach can ill afford to lose a scholarship athlete in midstream. At this point, I should add that I didn't find that the scholarship athletes were any more committed than well-motivated walk-ons. This really surprised me, since I expected scholarship students to be really gung-ho.

Along with the recruiting, time spent on the road was another drawback to coaching. This isn't as severe in track as it is in football or basketball, but aside from time spent recruiting, during the season quite a bit of time is spent competing away from school. Basically, I was (and still am) a homebody and didn't enjoy spending roughly two out of three weekends away from home during the season, which, by including cross country, ran from September to June. This was one of the things Lee Daniel and I had in common, and I figured that if someone like him could be a homebody, so could I.

As a coach, you have little real control over your success and failure. You hope that all the grandmothers of your team members are healthy on the dates of your big meets. Classroom teachers' failures are not in the newspaper like the losses of a coach.

Of course, there are plenty of plusses in coaching. The thrill of competition becomes engrained in an athlete, and most coaches are retired athletes. The person in school that can have the most positive influence on a teen-ager is usually the coach, and I cannot stress that enough. The coach and athlete spend a lot of time together under varying conditions (often trying), and the bonds between a coach and athlete are usually stronger than between a teacher and student, or a counselor and student. It is very important for the coach to realize this, and, along with everything else, accept being an important role model for his group of teens. A successful coach (being careful how we define successful) has a certain prestige in a community, which helps his rapport with the team.

After carefully considering all of the pros and cons I could apply to my situation, I decided it was time for me to retire from active coaching. Knowing myself better than anyone, I decided that I would be a better assistant coach than head coach. I told Moose that I didn't want to be considered for Alex's position. Soon after, Don Faley, a 1958 graduate of Notre Dame and a track monogram winner, was named head track coach. I stayed with Don for two years until he was able to bring in his own assistant, which he did in 1974.

In 1975, Joe Piane replaced Faley, and as of this date is still head track coach with an outstanding record. When Piane took over, I was asked to return to my position as assistant, but after thinking it over, I decided that 24 years was enough, and Joe needed someone with as much zip and pep as he had. I recommended Ed Kelly to him. Ed was a 1964 Notre Dame graduate and had earned three letters in track. Ed accepted, and served as an assistant for 10 years. I told him that the least he could do was to stay as long as I had. Ed did an excellent job with Joe.

My 30 years of being an athlete and coach ended. I followed it with seven years of starting high school track meets, both boys' and girls'.

A Surprise Return

Looking back, it is obvious that track played a major role in my life. Track was not a sport that I fantasized about as a child, like basketball and baseball. Those are the sports followed most by the media (along with football) and are the ones best understood by the public.

It wasn't until recently that summer track programs became available to children of all ages. They were not available when I was young. Many youngsters didn't go out for track until they tried and "failed" at the other sports. For many, it was the sport of last resort. I don't feel that is true today, due to the emphasis on track and the opportunities available. There is no excuse for a person not to participate today. Track being what it is, anyone can succeed by improving their personal bests, which is satisfying. Jogging for fitness, road races, and marathons give running publicity, which has increased its popularity.

Participation in track and field produces memories that give pleasure and benefits later in life. I have reached that point, and have expressed many of those memories in this book. Age and maturity have helped put the disappointments in their proper perspective, and the good memories have been a source of pleasure. Memories have to be relied upon, for if I go looking today for the places of my youth, this is what I find:

Central High School: gone, converted into apartments.
School Field track: gone, relocated outside the stadium.
Notre Dame Field house: gone, demolished.
Cartier Field: gone, provided the site for the Notre Dame library.
Riley High School: rebuilt north of the old site.
Old Riley track: gone, used for athletic facilities for the new Riley.

What is left? MEMORIES, lifelong relationships, and traditions of excellence that live on in new places, with new faces.

Afterword

I'm just doing my thing, something I created myself, and I'm proud to say that so far, nobody's been able to do anything about it.

Edwin Moses, Hurdler, Olympic Gold Medalist

After Alex Wilson's retirement, soon followed by my own, I thought my contact with Notre Dame track was over. Not so. Coach Joe Piane honored Alex by naming an indoor invitational meet after him, The Alex Wilson Invitational. While his health permitted, Alex and wife Mayme, returned for the meet and the reception that followed.

Track alumni were invited to attend, and many did. I was pleased for the opportunity once a year to maintain my track ties, to see the Wilsons, and to greet the returning track alumni. After Alex's health prevented his coming, the Alumni Reception still continued through 2005.

In 2006, Notre Dame and Joe Piane went a step further to celebrate 115 years of track at Notre Dame by holding a track reunion in conjunction with the Wilson Invitational. Activities were held over two days, culminating in a well-attended reception and dinner. Thanks to Athletic Director Kevin White and Coach Joe Piane, track at Notre Dame is alive and well. All track alumni should feel a sense of pride in their alma mater's track program, in what it was, what it is, and what it will be in the future.

Notre Dame track is part of me, and shall remain so. And I never left home.

Mayme and Alex Wilson, Bob Smith, and Martha Komora (daughter of former ND track coach, John Nicholson, who preceded Doc Handy).

Alex Wilson with Joe Piane, Notre Dame Head Track Coach

Appendix A
What is Track and Field ?

Anything good is developed slowly.
Sebastian Coe, Distance runner, Olympic Gold Medalist

Most people have a smattering of knowledge about track and field. A thorough knowledge is not necessary as long as the basics of organization and scoring are understood.

Track and field as a sport consists of running, jumping, and throwing. The running events take place on the track, and the throwing and jumping events take place in specially designated areas off the track. These are called field events. In a track meet the events are held in a specific order with a time schedule. Running and field events take place at the same time, so it requires a little practice to keep track of everything when watching a meet.

A meet may be organized between two schools or many schools, run by loosely organized summer park programs, or conducted within any association of smaller organizations, like the AAU (Amateur Athletic Union). The ultimate meet is the Olympic games, where the competition is between the countries of the world. Some meets are very formal and others are not. Sometimes the number of entrants is restricted.

Usually a team is limited in the number of entries in each event. This is something that is generally agreed upon by the teams

125

before the meet. The points awarded for each place in each event depends on the number of teams involved. In a dual meet, there are three places in each event. The scoring would be five points for first, three for second, and one for third. Ties are to be avoided, if possible. The method of determining ties would be decided before the meet by representatives of the competing teams. In the case of a tie, the points may be split. For example, if three tie for third in a dual meet, each athlete receives one third of a point. That is one way to do it.

A tie in the pole vault could be broken by agreeing that the vaulter with the fewest attempts wins. For example, it is agreed to start the competition at ten feet and that the bar be raised 6" each time. The vaulter gets three chances to clear each height and is out if he misses all three. In this example, three vaulters all cleared 12 feet. All three started at ten feet. Vaulter A cleared each height the first time, vaulting five times to clear 12 feet. "B" took ten vaults, and "C" took eight. All three made the final height. Since "A" had the fewest vaults, he finishes first. "C" finishes second, and "B" third. A good vaulter can "pass" any height to reduce the number of vaults taken. If he wants to start at 11 feet, he can, but he has to clear a height to score. If he starts at 11 feet and misses all three attempts, he is out.

In a dual meet, the relays score five points for first, with no points for second. There are four runners in a relay. The type of relay determines the distance each athlete runs. In the 4x400 relay, each runner runs 100 meters. In the 4x800 relay, each runner runs 200 meters. The baton is passed within a 20-meter exchange zone. Failure to do so results in disqualification.

In a triangular meet, there are four places, scoring 5-3-2-1. At larger meets, the relay points are doubled, and the scoring can vary, often with six places. Some meets are non-scoring. These meets are usually very early in the season or are meets that do not emphasize teams.

At indoor meets, the events are tailored to the size of the facility. The indoor sprint is either 60 or 70 meters. The 300 yard dash is a popular indoor event, as are the 600 and 1000.

An outdoor track usually has eight lanes. If there are more than eight entries, then trials are run. Each trial run is called a heat, and the number of heats depends on the number of entries. Usually, if there are two heats, the first four finishers from each heat qualify for the finals to fill an eight-lane track. Trials usually are run in the sprints and hurdles. The order of events is changed to include the trials and then the final. If the meet is large enough, the trials can be held one day and the finals the next. Whether trials are run or not can affect the way a coach places his team members.

At Notre Dame, in a normal dual meet, I would run the 100, 220, and the mile relay. At the Central Collegiate Conference meet held in Milwaukee, the trials were held in the afternoon and the finals at night. In this meet, I was entered in the 440 relay, the 100 and 220 yd. dashes. There were trials in all three events, so I would have a trial and final in the relay, trial and final in the 100, and a trial and final in the 220. The mile relay was the last event, and by the time the mile relay came along, I had run six races – 820 all-out sprinting yards. Coach Handy didn't use me in the mile relay. He found a fresher pair of legs.

The following are track and field events that are commonly included in a high school meet. The number of events an athlete may compete in depends on the meet. In a dual meet in high school, the limit is usually four.

Track events	Field events
100 meter dash	high jump
200 meter dash	long jump
400 meter dash	pole vault
800 meters	shot put
1600 meters	discus
3200 meters	
110 meter high hurdles	
300 meter low hurdles	
4x 200 meter relay	
4x 400 meter relay	

College events are quite similar, but many colleges include events that high schools don't, like the javelin throw and the hammer throw, which are too dangerous for high schools. The hammer is a four-foot cable with a handle on one end and a shot on the other. The hammer weighs 16 pounds and is thrown much like a discus from a ring 7 feet in diameter.

Track events that are run in larger meets are:
> 400 meter intermediate hurdles
> 3000 meter steeplechase (This event is run on the track with hurdles and water jumps.)
> Medley relays:
>> Sprint medley : 400-200-200-800
>> Distance medley: 400-800-1200-1600
> Other relays: 400m. relay, 800m. relay, 1600m. relay
> Longer distance races: 5000m., 10000m.
> Shuttle hurdle relay
> Field event: the triple jump. This is the hop, skip, and jump.

It would be very difficult to conduct a track meet without the officials. The number of officials depends on the size of the meet and the number of qualified officials available. It would help the track spectator to know who the officials are, where they are stationed, and their main duties.

The most obvious official is the starter, whose job it is to see to it that each race is started fairly.

Also found near the starting line is the Clerk of Course. This is a very important job, since the clerk calls up the events and assigns the lanes to the contestants. The assigned lanes in larger meets are usually drawn ahead of time. Once the runners are in place, the Clerk turns them over to the starter and then starts to line up the next race. How smoothly a meet runs depends largely on the Clerk of Course.

The timers and finish judges are at the finish line. The number of finish judges depends on the number of places to be awarded. There should be at least one judge for each place. Strangely, the easiest place to pick is first. Second, third, and fourth are harder because they are usually bunched together. This is especially true in the short sprints. The first place judge has precedence over the second place judge and the second over the third, etc. Ideally, more than one timer should time first place. In the case of conflicting times, the head timer determines the winning time.

The inspectors are stationed on each turn, looking for lane infractions and fouls. Any problem is reported to the referee, who makes the final decision as to disqualification, usually, following the recommendation of the inspector involved.

The referee is the final authority when decisions have to be made involving interpretation of rules, disqualifications, etc. Usually, the referee is a separate official, but in smaller meets, like high school dual meets, the role of the referee is combined with the starter.

Each field event has an event judge, who calls up contestants and keeps a record of each jump, vault, or throw. He also determines the final places of each contestant. The field event judge has to have a good knowledge of the rules and keep the event running smoothly.

A well-trained set of officials makes a meet run smoothly and enjoyable for the spectators to watch. A high school dual meet provides the interested fans continuous action for an hour and a half to two hours.

Appendix B
1944 Central High School Track

Coach: Bert Anson

Team:

Altgelt, Pat

Boyles, Bob (co-captain)

Chandonia, Dick

Easton, Don

Filley, Dick

Finger, Chuck

Green, Bob

Hood, Ernie

Kapalczynski, Ralph

Kendziorski, Len

Mathews, Joe (co-captain)

Matthews, Roland

Maciejewski, Jack

Mazurkiewicz, Gene

Neises, Chuck

Rossow, Eldon

Smith, Bob

Taylor, Richard

Yoder, Bill

The following results from the 1944 season include the events in which I participated:

Central 70 Riley 39 at School Field

100 yd. dash 1st **Smith (C)** 2nd Thomas (R) 3rd Taylor (C)
time :10.8

220 yd. dash 1st **Smith (C)** 2nd Thomas (R) 3rd Keiser (R)
time :24.0

880 yd. relay 1st **Central:** Kendziorski, **Smith,** Maciejewski, Mathews time 1:40.2

Mishawaka 66 Central 43 at Mishawaka

100 1st Mathews (C) 2nd **Smith (C)** 3rd Wardell (M)
time :10.8

220 1st **Smith (C)** 2nd DeBeck (M) 3rd Tagliaferri (M)
time :24.5

Adams 58 Central 51 at School Field

100 1st Fink (A) 2nd Mathews (C) 3rd Egendorfer (A)
time :11.1

220 1st McKinney (A) 2nd **Smith (C)** 3rd Fink (A) time :25.0

880 relay 1st **Central:** Kendziorski, **Smith,** Maciejewski,
Mathews time 1:41.1

City Meet at School Field: Adams 69.5 Central 45 Riley 26.5

100 1st Mathews (C) 2nd Fink (A) 3rd **Smith (C)** 4th
McEndorfer (A) time :11.2

220 1st Smith (C) 2nd Fink (A) 3rd McKinney (A) 4th Thomas
(R) time :23.7

880 relay 1st Adams 2nd **Central:** Kendziorski, **Smith,**
Maciejewski, Mathews time 1:38.8.

**Eastern Division at Mishawaka: Fort Wayne North 69.5
Elkhart 41.5 Mishawaka 39.5 Central 25 LaPorte 21.2 Adams
17.2 Goshen 13.6 Michigan City 4 Riley 1.4 Nappanee 0**

100 1st Morrow (FW) 2nd **Smith (C)** 3rd Fink (A) time :11

220 1st Longfellow (E) 2nd **Smith (C)** 3rd Miller (LP) time
:24.1

Northern Indiana Conference Finals at Mishawaka:
Hammond 58.704, Fort Wayne North 42, Mishwaka 24.87,
Elkhart 22.5, Central 10, Goshen 9.75, Gary Emerson 9, Gary
Froebel 8, East Chicago Washington 6.357, Valparaiso 6.357,
Adams 6, Gary Mann 5.25, E.C. Roosevelt 5, LaPorte 4.8,
Hammond Clark 3, Michigan City 2, Hammond Tech 1, Gary
Tolleston .857

100 1st Humphrey (H) 2nd Morrow (FW) 3rd Krueger (H) 4th
   Smith (C) 5th Miller(ECW) time :10.3
220 1st Lindholm (H) 2nd Grambo (H) 3rd Longfellow (E) 4th
   Perry (GM) 5th **Smith (C)** time :23.9

Sectional meet at Mishawaka: Mishawaka 41, Adams 31,
Central 21, LaPorte 16, Riley 9, Washington Clay 8,
Plymouth 6

100 1st Mathews (C) 2nd McDaniel (R) 3rd **Smith (C)**
   time :10.8
220 1st McKinney (A) 2nd Livinghouse (P) 3rd DeBeck (M)
   time :24.2
880 Relay 1st Mishawaka: Hickey, Tagliaferri, Wardell, DeBeck
   time 1:37

Appendix C
1945 Central High School Track

Coach: Jack Nash
Team:

Altgelt, Pat
Baughman, Charles (Tiny)
Brummond, Bill
Chandonia, Dick
Easton, Don
Hayes, Bill
Hepler, Al
Johnson, Jim
Maciejewski, Jack
Neises, Chuck

Nusshart, George
Newman, Don
Perkins, Leroy
Schleuder, Don
Smith, Bob (co-captain)
Taylor, Richard
Waters, Bob
Wilfing, Rudy
Yoder, Bill (co-captain)

Central 70 Riley 42 at School Field

100 1st **Smith (C)** 2nd Newman (C) 3rd Thomas (R) time :10.9
220 1st **Smith (C)** 2nd Newman (C) 3rd Thomas (R) time :23.6
880 Relay 1st **Central**: Newman, Schleuder, Taylor, **Smith**
     time 1:38.5

Central 61 Adams 48 at School Field

100 1st **Smith (C)** 2nd McKinney (A) 3rd Newman (C)
     time :11
220 1st **Smith (C)** 2nd McKinney (A) 3rd Schleuder (C)
     time :24.0
880 Relay 1st Adams - Central won but was disqualified.

134

Central 83 LaPorte 26 at LaPorte

100 1st **Smith (C)** 2nd Newman (C) 3rd Taylor (C) time :10.6

220 1st **Smith (C)** 2nd Newman (C) 3rd Kloss (LP) time :24.0

880 Relay 1st **Central:** Newman, Schleuder, Taylor, **Smith**
time 1: 39.9

Central 69.5 Plymouth 45.5 at Plymouth

Records are not available for this meet.

**City Meet: Central 51.5, Adams 38, Mishawaka 35.5, Riley 18
at School Field**

100 1st **Smith (C)** 2nd Newman (C) 3rd McKinney (A) 4th
Hickey (M) time :10.6

220 1st **Smith (C)** 2nd McKinney (A) 3rd Newman (C) 4th
Thomas (R) time :24.2

880 Relay 1st **Central:** Newman, Schleuder, Taylor, Smith,
time 1:36.2

**Eastern Division Conference at Mishawaka: Elkhart 55.5,
Fort Wayne North 49, Mishawaka 33, Adams 32.5, Central
31.5, Goshen 14.5, Riley 7, Michigan City 7, LaPorte 6,
Nappanee 3**

100 1st **Smith (C)** 2nd Newman (C) 3rd Owens (E) 4th Vogel
(FW) 5th Hickey (M) time :10.7

220 1st **Smith (C)** 2nd Vogel (FW) 3rd Hoffman (E) 4th
McKinney (A) 5th Miller (L) time :23.5

880 relay Central disqualified.

Northern Indiana Conference: Hammond 63.5, Gary Froebel 31, Gary Emerson 26, Elkhart 19, Central 14.5, Hammond Tech 12, Fort Wayne North 12, Adams 10.5, Hammond Clark 9, Mishawaka 7, Gary Wallace 5.5, Goshen 5, East Chicago Roosevelt 4.5, LaPorte 2, Michigan City 2, Whiting 1.5, East Chicago Washington 0, Valparaiso 0

100 1st Hanock (H) 2nd Morris (HC) 3rd Stroud (GF) 4th **Smith (C)** 5th Newman (C) time :10.6

220 1st Hanock (H) 2nd **Smith (C)** 3rd Morris (HC) 4th Maragos (GE) 5th Vogel (FWN) time :22.4

State Sectional: Adams 37, Central 32, LaPorte 14, Michigan City 13, North Judson 13, Plymouth 12, Mishawaka 9, Washington Clay 5

100 1st **Smith (C)** 2nd Newman (C) 3rd Hickey (M) time :10.7

220 1st **Smith (C)** 2nd McKinney (A) 3rd Danielson (P) time :23.5

880 Relay 1st **Central**: Newman, Schleuder, Taylor, **Smith** 2nd Adams 3rd Plymouth time 1:36.3

Appendix D
1947-1950 Notre Dame Track

These are meets and teams that Notre Dame met from 1947 through 1950 The exact years are not given; the purpose of the list is to indicate the caliber of competition Notre Dame met, week after week. Apart from the large meets, the schools listed were run in dual or triangular meets.

Indoor

Michigan State Relays
Central Collegiate Conference
Illinois Tech Relays
Chicago Daily News Relays
Purdue Relays
Purdue
Indiana
Missouri
Penn State
Michigan State
Bradley
Marquette
Iowa
Michigan AAU

Outdoor

Drake Relays
Kansas Relays
Indiana Big State
Cent. Collegiate Conf.
Indiana AAU
Michigan State
Pitt
Penn State
Missouri
Bradley
Marquette
Monmouth
Drake
Southern Relays
NCAA

Non-scoring Meets with no team title:

Chicago Daily News Relays (board track)

Michigan State Relays
Kansas Relays
Drake Relays

1947 Season

Indoor

Feb. 1   ND 65½   Purdue 38½

Feb. 8   Michigan State Relays

Feb. 15 ND 73½ Michigan Normal 30 Marquette 25½

Feb. 22 ND 67$^2/_3$ Iowa 43$^1/_3$

Mar. 1   Mich. State 61$^1/_3$ ND 52$^2/_3$

Mar. 8   Central Collegiate Conference 1st Michigan State 2nd ND

Mar.15 Illinois Tech Relays

Mar.22 Purdue Relays

Outdoor

Apr. 25 Drake Relays

May   3 Mich. State 76 ND 65

May 10 Indiana 77 ND 52 Purdue34

May 17 ND 60 Purdue 57 Northwestern 39

May 24 Big State Meet IN 75½ ND 71$^5/_6$ Purdue 56

May 31 ND 79 Bradley 48½ Marquette 36½

June   7 Central Collegiate Conference 1st Michigan State
         2nd Illinois 3rd Wisconsin 4th ND

1948 Season

Indoor

Feb. 7   Michigan State Relays

Feb. 20   Missouri 65 ND 49

Feb. 28   Penn State 58½ ND 52½

Mar. 6   Central Collegiate Conference 1st Michigan State 2nd ND

Mar. 13 Illinois Tech Relays

Mar. 27 Purdue Relays

Outdoor

Apr. 23 Drake Relays

May   1 ND 89 Bradley 55 Drake 30

May   8 ND 93 Marquette 48

May 15 Michigan State 74 ND 67

May 22 Big State Meet ND 83 Indiana 73 Purdue 48

June   5 Indiana AAU 1st ND

June 11 Central Collegiate Conference 1st Illinois 2nd ND 3rd
     Michigan State

June 19 NCAA Meet in Minneapolis

July 9-10 Final Olympic Trials - Minneapolis

1949 Season

Indoor

Jan. 28 Michigan AAU

Feb.   5 Michigan State Relays

Feb. 19 ND 69 Purdue 45

Feb. 25 ND 83 Bradley 31

Mar.   5 Central Collegiate Conference 1st Michigan State 2nd
     Michigan Normal 3rd ND

Mar.12 Illinois Tech Relays

Mar. 26 Purdue Relays

Outdoor

Apr. 8-9 Southern Relays

Apr. 23   Mich.State 85 ND 56

Apr. 30   Drake Relays

May   7   ND $86^2/_3$ Pitt $44^1/_3$

May 14   ND 67 Missouri 64

May 21   Penn State 69 ND 62

May 28 Big State Meet ND 72½   Indiana 66½   Purdue 57

June 4 Central Collegiate Conference 1st Michigan State 2nd ND

June 17-18 NCAA meet in Los Angeles

1950 Season

Indoor

Feb. 4 Michigan State Relays

Feb. 11 ND 66½ Missouri 47½

Feb. 18 ND 64½ Purdue 49½

Feb. 25 ND 63 Indiana 51

Mar. 4 Central Collegiate Conference 1st Michigan State 2nd ND

Mar. 11 Illinois Tech Relays

Mar. 18 Chicago Daily News Relays

Mar. 25 Purdue Relays

Outdoor

Apr. 22 Kansas Relays

Apr. 28-29 Drake Relays

May 6 Pitt 65$^2/_3$ ND 65$^1/_3$

May 12 Michigan State 83 ND 58

May 19 Big State Meet Indiana 104½ ND 60 Purdue 56½

May 27 Closed Central Collegiates ND 89 Marquette 50
      Bradley 46 Drake 20

June 3 ND 75 Bradley 63 Monmouth 25

June 10 Open Central Collegiate Conference

Notes:

When I was in school, Michigan State was Michigan State College. Later it became Michigan State University. Michigan Normal became Eastern Michigan University.

Scores were not available for all scored meets.

The Central Collegiate Conference was formed in 1926 by Knute Rockne of Notre Dame, Ralph Young of Michigan State, and Conrad Jennings of Marquette. It was formed in response to the Western Conference (Big Ten) limiting participants in their conference meet to Big Ten schools. That left many athletes without a big meet in the late Spring that they could use as a warm up for the NCAA and other prominent summer meets. Rockne, Young, and Jennings formed the Central Collegiate Conference as an open meet for primarily midwest athletes to fill the void created by the actions of the Big Ten. Member schools were: Bradley, Butler, DePaul, Detroit, Drake, Loyola, Marquette, Michigan Normal, Michigan State, Notre Dame, Wayne State, and Western Michigan.

Appendix E
South Bend Riley H.S. Track –
Top Performances from
1951 through 1958

100 yard dash

Ron Walling	:10.2	1956
Gary Monus	:10.3	1955
Jerry Grabill	:10.4	1951
Paul Pozil	:10.4	1955

220 yard dash

Ron Walling	:22.5	1956
John Abell	:23.2	1953
Paul Pozil	:23.5	1955

440 yard dash

Larry Pahl	:52.5	1955
Jack Kudlaty	:52.9	1952
Bob Daniels	:54.0	1951
Paul Pozil	:54.0	1955

880 yard dash

Ralph Long	2:01.8	1952
Tom Baughman	2:02.7	1958
Jim Mahoney	2:05	1953

Mile Run

Louis Cass	4:38.7	1957
Bill Manuszak	4:39.5	1955
Phil Harris	4:47.0	1952

Pole Vault

Dick Liechty	12' 3"	1953
Don Katona	11' 3"	1957
Ed Willamowski	10' 9"	1952

High Hurdles
* state champion

John Abell	:14.8	1954*
Dick Whitaker	:15.5	1953
Nick Medich	:15.8	1951

Low Hurdles

John Abell	:19.7	1954*
Burnie Maurek	:20.6	1955
Phil Grundy	:21.8	1958

High Jump   **Long Jump**

Dick Whitaker   6' 1¾" 1953   Gary Monus   21'4"   1955

Chuck Kalwitz   5'11³/₈"1955   Chuck Kalwitz   20' 11½"   1955

George Page   5'10" 1958   Sam Kambol   20' 6¼"   1951

Shot Put

Jerry Jacobs   50' 3 ¾"   1952

Mike Bingaman   48'1"   1955

Dave Ton   44'11"   1958

Mile Relay

Larry Pahl, Ed Payton, Paul Pozil, Pete Holmgren   3:30.6 1954

Jack Kudlaty, Jim Mahoney, Ralph Long, Emil Toth 3:35.5 1952

Paul Pozil, Pete Holmgren, Bill Thrasher, Larry Pahl 3:37.7 1956

880 Relay

Jack Kudlaty, Joe Meszaras, Chuck Kalwitz, John Abell
                          1:33.9 1954

Kudlaty, Kalwitz, Meszaras, Abell 1:34.3 1954

Kudlaty, Meszaras, Kalwitz, Abell 1:34.8 1954

Appendix F
Riley High School Cross Country
1951-1957

Won-Lost records are given for dual meets only. Each runner's position on the lists below signifies his average order of finish on Riley's team at the end of the season.

1951	1952
Won 6 Lost 5	**Won 7 Lost 4 Tied 1**
1. Jim Lakatos	1. Phil Harris
2. Bob Daniels	2. Tom Swem
3. Chuck Carr	3. Tom Priddy
4. Lee Snodgrass	4. Chuck McGeath
5. Phil Harris	5. Marvin Wallace
6. Ed Willamowski	6. Jim Mahoney
7. Marvin Wallace	7. Roger Overmyer

1953	1954
Won 8 Lost 4	**Won 12 Lost 2**
1. Bill Manuszak	1. Bill Manuszak
2. Jim Smith	2. Roger Overmyer
3. Dan Post	3. Jim Smith
4. Roger Overmyer	4. Ken Jackson
5. Ken Jackson	5. Ken Ford
6. Ernie Hoover	6. Louie Cass
7. Fred Bird	7. Dave Fritz

1955	1956
Won 10 Lost 2	**Won 11 Lost 1**
1. Dave Fritz	1. Louie Cass
2. Louie Cass	2. Dave Fritz
3. Jim Smith	3. Rodger McKee
4. Richard Lewis	4. Jim Manuszak
5. Larry Pahl	5. Ken Selby
6. Jim Manuszak	6. Bill Barnes
7. Ken Jackson	7. Larry Severin

1957
Won 8 Lost 7
1. Leon Copeland
2. Bill Barnes
3. George Page
4. Herman West
5. Don Hanish
6. Larry Severin
7. Tom Baughman

APPENDIX G
Notre Dame Track and Field
Records - 1958 through 1972

Outdoor Records

100 meter dash	:10.2	Bill Hurd	1969
100 yard dash	:09.3	Bill Hurd	1969
200 meter dash	:20.5	Bill Hurd	1969
880 yard dash	1:48.2	Joe Quigley	1969
120 yard High Hurdles	:13.5	Tom McMannon	1971
440 yard relay	:40.7	Ole Skarstein, Jack Samar, Tom Buckley, Bill Hurd	1969
880 yard relay	1:25.1	Ole Skarstein, Bob Timm, Doug Breunlin, Bill Hurd	1968
Mile relay	3:10.7	Paul Gough, Doug Breunlin, Joe Quigley, Bill Hurd	1969
Sprint Medley relay	3:16.0	Ole Skarstein, Doug Breunlin, Bill Hurd, Joe Quigley	1968
Discus	191' 7¾"	Paul Gill	1970
Shot	59' 5¾"	Greg Cortina	1972
Javelin	224'10½"	Tom Morando	1958

Indoor Records

300 yard dash	:29.8	Bill Hurd	1968
440 yard dash	:47.9	Bill Boyle	1964
600 yard dash	1:09.4	Rick Wohlhuter	1969
880 yards	1:49.3	Pete Ferrell	1967
1000 yd.	2:09.0	Ed Dean	1966
		Joe Quigley	1969
Shot	60' 10 ½"	Greg Cortina	1972
Shuttle Hurdle Relay	:28.4	Mike Dimick, Tom McMannon, Dave Stickler, Joe Utz	1971

About the Author

Robert C. Smith was born in South Bend, Indiana in 1927, and has lived there all his life, except for his time in the navy. He lived in the same house from birth until his marriage in 1950. He attended Muessel School from kindergarten through 9th grade, went on to Central High School, and got his Bachelor of Science degree in Physical Education from the University of Notre Dame in 1950.

While at Notre Dame, he won four monograms in track and was named Notre Dame All-American in 1948. He is a Monogram Club member. His senior year, he served as team captain, the first South Bend resident ever elected.

He graduated from Indiana University in 1953 with a M.S. in Education, with additional graduate work at Purdue and Indiana University and two summers at Notre Dame in the Biology Department, doing research with the Mosquito Genetics Project.

Bob Smith was head track and cross country coach at Riley High School in South Bend before serving as assistant track coach at Notre Dame for 16 years. In 1995 he was inducted into the Riley Athletic Hall of Fame as a coach.

Bob taught for 39 years in the South Bend School Corporation: 29 years at Riley High School and 10 years at Jackson when it was a high school. He taught General Science and first and second year Biology. He served as Science Department Chairman at both Jackson and Riley for a total of eighteen years.

He was assistant track coach at Notre Dame from 1958 to 1974.

Printed in the United States
88455LV00009BA/182/A